PROFILES OF VALOR

3

Character Studies
from the
War of Independence

Marilyn Boyer &
Grace Tumas Ehrman

Master Books First Printing: November 2025
Second Printing: May 2026

Master Books, P.O. Box 726, Green Forest, AR 72638

Master Books® is a division of the New Leaf Publishing Group, LLC.

ISBN: 978-1-68344-427-5
ISBN: 978-1-61458-946-4 (digital)

All Scripture verses are from the King James Version of the Bible.

Please consider requesting that a copy of this volume be purchased by your local library system.

Printed in the United States of America

PROFILES OF VALOR

Character Studies from the War of Independence

December 1777 – October 1780

Credits

Thanks to the following people for their investment in helping to preserve these inspiring stories from America's past. It is my prayer that their efforts will reap a bountiful harvest as these stories will serve to be an inspiration to those in whose hands America's future lies!

I wish to thank David Barton, who has been such an inspiration to me, personally, to become excited about learning about our godly heritage. God has gifted him for such a time as this in our country. He is the master of primary source documents! Tuesday night has traditionally been "Barton night" in our home as we gather to watch his DVDs and invite friends in to learn with us! It is only as we get truth back into the public square that we can hope to preserve the heritage of freedom handed down to us.

Thanks to Grace Tumas Ehrman, for her role in crafting these stories in such a way that they are a delight to read! It's great when even the editors have to read the stories first to see what happens and then go back and edit!

Thanks to my dear friend Mary Ann Edman who is the world's most efficient multi-tasker, committed to producing quality that will be a tribute to our

Lord and Savior. Her creativity has been indispensable in producing the layout and graphic design for this book as well as editing the mistakes the rest of us overlooked!

Thanks to Judy Saunders, my long-time friend and prayer warrior, for her faithful work in the tedious editing process. God has gifted her with a precise eye for detail. She sees things I just don't notice. Thanks, my friend!

Thanks to my son, Rick, who, despite his incredibly busy life, has read these stories to his children at night, while editing each for accuracy of content to assure we are portraying these men and women in an worthy manner, giving honor where honor is due.

Chronological Table of Contents

Table of Contents by Character Quality

Introduction

Throughout the struggle for independence, the Founding Fathers acknowledged God moving on their behalf. Some of those occasions are referenced in the stories included in this book.

The colonists were fighting for freedom against the most powerful, well-trained, and well-financed country in the world. They acknowledged many times that the Hand of Providence worked on their behalf. It was customary for Congress to appoint days of fasting and prayer in giving thanks to God for His direct intervention. Even a British general was known to comment that it seemed an invisible hand was working on behalf of the colonists.

John Adams declared, "The general principles on which the fathers achieved independence were … the general principles of Christianity."[1]

Issac Potts, a Quaker man, happened upon George Washington kneeling in the snow crying out in anguish to God for protection and provision for his army. Potts, who had previously thought that a man could not be both a Christian and a soldier, was greatly moved by the intensity and sincerity of the prayer.

George Washington in his inaugural address commented, "No people can be bound to acknowledge and adore the Invisible Hand, which conducts in the affairs of men more than the people of the United States. … Every step, by which they have been advanced to the character of an independent nation, seems to have been distinguished by some token of providential agency… ."[2]

In this book you will learn about real-life examples of bravery, compassion, loyalty, alertness, boldness, and incredible persistence. God accomplishes His purposes through men and women who seek to be useful and who lay aside their own comfort to accomplish great tasks.

How great a heritage we have forgotten! My hope is that this book will arm you with truth to share with others as you do your part to defend that freedom today.

Marilyn Boyer

Commitment

DEFINITION

Devoting myself to act upon my promises

MEMORY VERSE

Commit thy way unto the LORD; trust also in him; and he shall bring it to pass.

Psalm 37:5

Frenchman's War

Marquis de Lafayette

France

August 8, 1775

The young man's green eyes glowed with excitement as he listened. Outside, the warm summer air poured in from the green lawns of the chateau at Auvergne. As Prince William Henry, the Duke of Gloucester, spoke about the American Revolution in clipped, British tones, the tall, red-haired, nineteen-year-old Marquis de Lafayette felt a fresh wind blowing from across the sea. He could see the tattered little Continental army, led by Washington, struggling for freedom against a world superpower. His

The Marquis de Lafayette

sympathy overwhelmed him. One of the richest men in France, the Marquis did not fit in at the court of Louis XVI. He felt awkward in his elegant dragoon uniform. He never knew what to say. Unable to stay at his chateau with his beloved, eighteen-year-old wife, Adrianne, while a war for independence raged,

Lafayette decided to set out at once for America. "At the first news of this quarrel," he exclaimed, "my heart was enrolled in it."

He knew that Louis XVI, distantly related to Adrianne, would disapprove of his adventure. Secretly, he whispered his plan to his friend the Comte de Broglie and the Baron Johan de Kalb. Meeting with Silas Deane, an American agent in Paris in December 1776, the three men received written agreements that they would become major generals as soon as they stepped on American soil. Louis XVI flatly forbade the Marquis de Lafayette to leave France. In April, Lafayette slipped past the king's guards and boarded a ship in the Bordeaux harbor. When the news of his escape arrived in Paris, the British ambassador threatened war unless the king seized Lafayette's ship and brought him back. Louis immediately sent men with *letters de cachet* to arrest the Marquis. Placed in custody, Lafayette climbed into a disguise and fled to his ship with seven other French officers. When they put out to sea, two British cruisers set off after them. Lafayette and his men quickly put distance between them, watching the Royal Navy grow smaller until they disappeared. After a weary voyage of almost two months, the Marquis landed on the coast off Georgetown, South Carolina.

When he reached Philadelphia, Congress met him with cold silence. Tired of "French glory seekers,"

Congress refused to give Lafayette a major generalship. Eagerly, the Marquis offered to serve without pay. As the weeks passed with no result, the Frenchman almost packed up and started for home. Then one day, a letter from Benjamin Franklin in Paris landed on Washington's desk. Franklin described how people loved the Marquis de Lafayette in France, and begged Washington to take the young man on as an aide-de-camp.

Washington agreed. The two men met for dinner at the Philadelphia City Tavern on July 31, 1777. Together, they discussed the situation. At this point, Washington had only about 11,000 Continental soldiers. They had few supplies, poor equipment, and faced harassment from British troops. Gladly accepting the post on Washington's staff, Lafayette soon became Washington's information officer, gathering intelligence for the army. Lafayette set out on a successful mission to negotiate an alliance with the Oneida Nation against the British. When he appeared again at Valley Forge, he came up against the "Conway Cabal," a group of high-ranking officers that tried to turn Congress against Washington and strip him of his title as Commander-in-Chief. When members of the cabal approached Lafayette for his support, he turned them down, declaring his unwavering commitment to Washington as a friend and a leader. Washington, in turn, appreciated Lafayette's abilities as a sober strategist and a commander.

Washington and Lafayette at Valley Forge

Before long, Washington began to treat the Marquis like his own son.

Lafayette saw his first action in the colonies at the Battle of Monmouth in June 1777. In the autumn, he fell with a wounded leg while trying to rally the Third Pennsylvania Brigade at Brandywine on September 11. The Marquis refused to let a doctor touch him until he had organized the troops into an orderly retreat. Due to his unwavering commitment to the cause, Washington recommended his promotion to Major General. Over the next few months, the Frenchman assisted Major General Nathanael Greene on his campaign through New Jersey.

On June 19, 1778, the British evacuated Philadelphia and set off across New Jersey with Washington's generals in hot pursuit. Catching up with the British forces, Washington ordered "Light Horse Harry" Lee to attack and strike them in the rear. After the first assault, Washington would throw in the rest of the army to defeat Cornwallis' troopers. By the time Washington and Lafayette caught up to Lee, they found him tumbling back in full retreat. Riding into the middle of the combat, Washington stopped the retreat, organized the ranks, and turned the men back to face the enemy. The second attack succeeded. The British fell back, but the setting sun

Lafayette rallies the troops at Brandywine

streaked woods and fields. Faced with approaching darkness, Washington could not gain a decisive victory. He placed the men in position, planning to attack again at first light. During the night, the British stealthily slipped away and retreated into New York.

Meanwhile, Lafayette worked tirelessly as a peacemaker, patching up Franco-American relations in the Continental Army. When a riot broke out between the French fleet under Admiral d'Estaing and the Americans, Lafayette hastened to smooth things over. Seriously concerned about the strength of the alliance, Lafayette asked for permission to return to France to lobby for more money and troops, departing in 1779.

"Serving America is to my heart an inexpressible happiness," the Marquis wrote, sailing joyfully back to the colonies on the *Hermione* in May, 1780. With him came 6,000 fresh troops commanded by General Jean-Baptiste de Rochambeau. Lafayette privately explained to Rochambeau that they could only achieve military success if the French and Americans maintained a harmonious relationship. With these fresh troops behind them, Washington and Rochambeau began plotting the final campaign to assure independence.

In July 1781, Lord Cornwallis, retreating from the Carolinas, received orders to divide his troops, sending some of them to New York and setting the others to establishing a defensive position in

Signing the Treaty of Paris which ended the war

Virginia. Moving cautiously down the Yorktown Peninsula, Cornwallis soon faced the Chesapeake Bay. Washington, still camped at West Point, feared that Cornwallis intended to stage an attack on Philadelphia from the peninsula. He sent word to Lafayette to pull 2,000 troops together. By advancing on the peninsula and stringing his men out along the coast, Lafayette hoped to keep Cornwallis bottled up at Yorktown until Washington and Rochambeau could arrive. The Marquis had already spent over half of his own fortune to feed, clothe, and equip the Continental soldiers. Now, he borrowed heavily from Baltimore merchants in order to provide his men with necessary food, shoes, and clothing.

Lafayette also knew that he had reinforcements coming from the French colonies in the Caribbean. On August 30, Admiral Francois-Joseph-Paul, the Comte de Grasse, sailed into the blue waters of the Chesapeake Bay. The lily flags of six French frigates and twenty-eight battleships, filled with 15,000 sailors and 3,100 marines, streamed against the horizon.

Lafayette visits Washington at Mount Vernon in 1784

Soon Lafayette faced the British with 5,500 regular French troops and 3,000 militiamen. Cornwallis had 8,800 British, Loyalist, and Hessian troops inside the fortifications. When Washington arrived in September, Lafayette's men laid siege to Yorktown on October 6th. Keeping up a steady watch offshore, the French fleet prevented Cornwallis from breaking through Lafayette's encircling lines and escaping by sea. De Grasse's ships also kept Cornwallis from sending for help or receiving reinforcements from Howe in New York. Cut off from supplies, Cornwallis finally surrendered on October 19th, rather than let his men starve to death.

Lafayette, trim and upright in his French uniform, watched as the British signed the Treaty of Paris that signaled the end of the war. After almost four continuous years in America, Lafayette prepared to sail home to his wife, Adrianne, on December 23, 1781. From his estate at Mount Vernon, Washington admitted his high regard for his young staff officer. "I owe it to your friendship and to my affectionate regard for you, my dear Marquis, not to let you leave this country without carrying with you … new expressions of the high sense I entertain of your military conduct and other important services in the course of the last campaign, although the latter are too well known to need the testimony of my approbation." From aboard ship, the Marquis replied wistfully: "Adieu, my dear General; I know your heart so well that I am sure that no distance can alter your attachment to me. With the same candour I assure that my love, respect and my gratitude for you, are above expression; that, at the moment of leaving you, I felt more than ever the strength of those friendly ties that forever bind me to you."

Three years later, the Marquis and Adrianne

spent eleven blissful days with Washington at Mount Vernon in August 1784. Washington and Lafayette would never see each other again. Dark clouds loomed on the horizon. Within a few years, Washington reluctantly left Mount Vernon to shoulder his duties as President of the United States. Lafayette headed into the turbulent days of the French Revolution as a freedom fighter, an advocate of freedom of speech and religion, and a champion for freed slaves in the French colonies. During the French Revolution, Lafayette sent the keys of the Bastille Prison to President Washington as an expression of liberty. Later, he faced prison and destitution, but he never regretted fighting for freedom.

The Marquis de Lafayette demonstrated his commitment to freedom and the American colonies by devoting his life and his fortune to their welfare. "How have I loved liberty?" Lafayette exclaimed. "With the enthusiasm of religion, with the rapture of love, with the conviction of geometry: that is how I have always loved liberty."

He devoted himself, his life, his fortune, his hereditary honors, his towering ambition, his splendid hopes, all to the cause of liberty. He came to another hemisphere to defend her. He became one of the most effective champions of our Independence; but, that once achieved, he returned to his own country, and thenceforward took no part in the controversies which have divided us.

—John Quincy Adams,
in an eulogy of the Marquis de Lafayette

Questions

1. What did Lafayette say was his attitude the moment he heard of the conflict of the colonists?
2. Who was Lafayette?
3. What difficulties did Lafayette encounter in being able to leave France to assist America?
4. How did Congress first greet Lafayette?
5. What changed their mind?
6. Tell of Washington's first meeting with Lafayette. How did he come to treat Lafayette?
7. Where did Lafayette see his first action in battle? What display of bravery and commitment did he demonstrate at this battle?
8. How did Lafayette work as a peacemaker?
9. What did Lafayette proclaim about serving America?
10. Tell of Lafayette's involvement in the Battle of Yorktown.
11. Tell of the special relationship shared between Washington and Lafayette.
12. What did Lafayette say which demonstrated his commitment to America and to freedom?

May the friends of America rejoice! May her enemies be humbled and her censors silenced at the news of her noble exertions in continuance of those principles which have placed her so high in the annals of history and among the nations of the earth.

—Marquis de Lafayette,
in a letter to John Jay, 30 May 1787

13. What things are there in your life to which you could demonstrate commitment? What plans can you make to put this into practice?

Discretion

DEFINITION

Avoiding any words, actions,
or attitudes
that could give the appearance of evil

MEMORY VERSE

For his God doth instruct him to
discretion, and doth teach him.
Isaiah 28:26

The Petticoat Spy

Nancy Strong

Long Island, New York

1778

There was a wind today. It billowed across Setauket Sound and ruffled the sea-grass, tugging at Anna "Nancy" Strong's skirt. British soldiers had overrun Setauket, turning the local Presbyterian Church into a barracks and tearing out the gravestones to build a wall around the garrison. General Washington, pushed out of New York by successive British victories, had regrouped his men across the river in New Jersey and Delaware. Alone with her seven children on an isolated plantation out on Strong's Neck, thirty-seven-year-old Nancy felt open to British marauders who frequently attacked and set fire to lonely houses. To avoid danger, she moved to a little cottage across Conscience Bay from Thomas Woodhull's farm. From there, she could keep an eye on the big manor house now swarming with Redcoats.

She had seen Redcoats today. Stooping, she chose a black petticoat and carefully pinned it in the center of the clothesline. Unlike her usual red petticoat, the black cloth square flapped like a signal towards the cove. She could feel eyes pricking her back, watching her, each time she came out with a basket of laundry under her arm. But there was nothing to see: only a young woman hanging out the daily wash. In one of the coves, Lieutenant Caleb Brewster, code name Agent 725, crouched in his navy whaleboat waiting for the all-clear signal from Nancy.

The Setauket or Culper Spy Ring stretched from New York City all the way to Washington's headquarters and back. In New York City, Robert Townsend, a patriot who owned a coffee shop near Wall Street, masqueraded as a Tory and chatted with British generals over afternoon drinks. Then he wrote down the information and passed them on to the next agent.

The British suspected any colonist dressed in civilian clothes as a spy, so anyone passing through

British lines needed a good reason to do so. Nancy Strong filled out large orders for supplies and gave them to twenty-nine-year-old East Setauket tavern-keeper, Captain Austin Roe. Roe rode the fifty-five miles into New York City, casually dodging British troops and highwaymen. Tired and dusty, Roe arrived at Townsend's coffee house and silently handed him a letter. It read simply: "I wish you to send by bearer _ ream of letter paper." Stepping into his quarters, Townsend opened a closet, unscrewed the lid of a bottle he kept there and carefully brushed the fluid over the letter. A second message sprang out of the paper. General Washington requested information about British plans. When Townsend

Whaleboat of the kind used by the Culper Spy Ring

Major Benjamin Tallmadge

glanced out, he found that Captain Roe had crossed the street to the printer James Rivington. A few minutes later Roe reappeared, carrying a half ream of paper under his arm. In Townsend's rooms once more, the two men peeled open the package so gently that it could be resealed without showing that it had ever been opened. Next, Townsend started counting the sheets of paper. When he arrived at a certain number they had already agreed upon, he slipped it out. Bending over the table, he selected another bottle, dipped in his quill and began writing a letter to Washington. As the ink dried, the writing vanished. Townsend inserted the sheet into the same place and resealed the package.

Captain Roe strode outside, stuffed his saddlebags with purchases and set out for the Brooklyn Ferry. Completing the exhausting one hundred ten-mile round-trip in time to milk the cows, Roe stopped by his pasture next to Thomas Woodhull's farm. The captain slid the package into a drop box hidden behind the fence and moved on.

Nancy, watching from Strong's Neck, saw that the information had arrived. When she hung out a black petticoat, her seventeen-year-old neighbor, Thomas Woodhull, knew that he could now safely contact Caleb Brewster. Woodhull could not see Brewster from his house, so he had to rely on Nancy's homemade signals from the clothesline. Woodhull's job was to make sure that the information delivered to Washington came from a reliable source. He also kept track of everyday operations and often risked his life to hunt for information in New York City and west of Long Island. So far, the British had identified only Caleb Brewster as a spy.

Meanwhile, Caleb Brewster lay low in his whaleboat, straining his eyes to see the signal that would tell him in which cove he could safely moor his boat. Nancy managed to keep it a dark secret how she knew just when Caleb Brewster had hidden on her property. Outlined against the sky, Nancy kept methodically hanging up handkerchiefs. Brewster stared at the code formation. Three handkerchiefs today. The Culper Spy Ring had given each of the six coves a designated number. It was safe to go to cove Number Three. He slipped his oars into the oarlocks and pushed off softly. Thomas Woodhull waited for him among the tangled trees at the edge of the shoreline. From there, Brewster rowed across the Sound where he turned the message in to Major Tallmadge's headquarters in unoccupied Connecticut. The head of the spy ring, Benjamin Tallmadge, code name John Bolton, passed information from Washington to the patriots and from Caleb Brewster back to the Continental Army.

Another contact had been made safely. If Nancy closed her eyes, she could see her husband lying handcuffed in the filthy hold of the British prison ship, the *Jersey*. Once, she rowed out to the ship in a dinghy stuffed with food. In the dim light, she saw her husband's aristocratic white face and knew that he could not live long in this place. Both sides rarely offered parole to prisoners. While her Tory relatives worked successfully to bribe the British authorities for her husband's release and safe harbor in Connecticut, Nancy did everything she could to make sure that the British occupying New York did not succeed. Carefully, she chose a red petticoat and hung it on the line. Then she picked up her basket and returned to the house. It would be the same next week. And the week after.

Nancy Strong's clothesline

The Setauket or Culper spy network proved so successful that their activities led to the capture of Benedict Arnold's British spy Major Andre. In addition, the ring smuggled information through to Washington that enabled him to stop the British from capturing Newport, Rhode Island, and prevented the annihilation of the French fleet. For five years, not a single member of the Culper spy ring was ever caught operating right under the nose of the British in New York. Nancy Strong and the other members of the group displayed such discretion that the depth of their contribution to the cause of independence was not discovered until the twentieth century.

Questions

1. How did Nancy Strong demonstrate discretion?
2. What information did she pass on to the Continentals?
3. What did the color and number of the petticoats signify?
4. Where was Nancy's husband?
5. How do we know that the members of this spy ring successfully practiced discretion?
6. What are some things you could do to practice discretion in your life?
7. If you hung around with others who were doing something wrong, would you be showing discretion? Can you think of a verse in Proverbs that talks about choosing friends wisely?

Compassion

DEFINITION

Investing whatever is necessary to meet the needs of others

MEMORY VERSE

And if thou draw out thy soul to the hungry, and satisfy the afflicted soul; then shall thy light rise in obscurity, and thy darkness be as the noonday.

Isaiah 58:10

Lady Liberty

Martha Washington

Valley Forge, Pennsylvania
February 1778

Her small foot touched the wet snow as she stepped down from the carriage that had brought her to this valley. She glanced up at the dark Schuylkill Mountains that ringed in the camp. A short distance away, yellow lamplight gleamed from army headquarters. As she entered Isaac Potts' house, her "dearest" started up from the table where he sat writing yet another hopeless letter to Congress. His weary, lined face broke into a smile. Her eyes ran over his tall figure and broad shoulders encased in the buff-and-blue coat of the Continental Army. In a few days, General George Washington would turn forty-five, and Martha Washington had arrived in time to celebrate his birthday.

Martha Washington

There was little else to celebrate. Threatened by British forces and unable to impose taxes on the scattered thirteen colonies, Congress could not provide its struggling army with either food or clothing. Washington wrote to them desperately again and again, reminding them that only the army stood between the colonies and domination once more by Great Britain.

Driving over the roads covered with slippery snow that continually melted and froze again, Martha Washington arrived at the main encampment. As she stepped out of the carriage, figures moved slowly towards her through the trees like the tattered ghosts of an army.

Martha gestured to the line of carriages that rolled down the road behind her. Bursting with medicine, food, cloth, wool, and sewing materials, the newly arrived carriages seemed like Christmas trees to the hungry soldiers. When Martha entered the split-slab huts, daubed with clay to keep out the cold, she found that the soldiers had built even the fireplaces out of wood. The walls were low, only six-and-a-half feet high. In the darkness, Martha could make out the shadows of sick soldiers lying on wretched straw pallets. Many of them had no shoes. Ragged soldiers cooking on the hearth glanced up as she came in. Today they actually had something to cook. Without any utensils, they mixed a handful of coarse corn flour with cold water and patted it onto a flat stone. While the corn-cake turned brown, another soldier broiled a scrap of beef on a stick over the fire. Often, soldiers told her, their rations consisted of a single bowl of beef stew swimming with burnt leaves and dirt. Although the officers' huts stood behind the line of soldiers' cabins, desertion ran high among both rank and file that winter.

Almost 2,000 out of 11,000 men had already died.

Deeply moved with compassion for these men, Martha immediately went to work. Her experience running Mount Vernon during the war had given her excellent administrative skills. She looked over the schedules for planting crops and gardens. She directed meal-planning and even oversaw the work of sixteen spinning wheels in the plantation's workshop.

From her headquarters at the Potts' house, Martha organized the Women's Relief Squad. Sarah Alexander, Lady Stirling, Mrs. Clement Biddle, Mrs. Henry Knox and a number of other army wives met every day to knit socks, mittens, and caps for the men struggling through the snow a short distance away at camp. Cheerfully, they mended torn and lice-filled coats and trousers, and sewed new shirts while General Washington again took up his quill to write to Congress for supplies. "My men," he pleaded, gazing out the window, "are leaving bloody tracks in the snow."

The Women's Relief Squad only rested on Sunday. Martha herself worked till long after dark, straining her eyes in the dim, flickering candlelight to throw one stitch over another. Martha even skimped on her personal appearance, sometimes even using thorns instead of pins to fasten her dress. When the friendly Oneida Nation donated more than six hundred bushels of dried corn to the white soldiers starving nearby, they also taught the officers' wives how to cook it.

General Washington's birthday fell in February.

Martha with her husband at Valley Forge

Somehow, Martha managed to organize a small party to cheer him up. The meal was bare and simple. That week, famine stalked the camp, so that even the commander-in-chief had little to eat. The few army officers and wives invited listened to a special concert performed by the fifes and drums of the

Second Continental Artillery. They had showed up at headquarters without invitation on the General's birthday. Afterwards, Martha went up to the musicians and thanked them on her husband's behalf. Then she pressed fifteen shillings into their hands.

Martha took care of the General with calm protectiveness. Now she no longer had to worry about his letters being intercepted by the British or fear that he had forgotten to write. She oversaw most of the household cares, freeing his day up for more important work. She made sure that the household ran smoothly, that he had clean clothes and snowy linen. She planned meals for his officers and aides-de-camp who discussed the fate of the army, Congress, and summer campaigns against the British. Inspired by her example, the other wives threw small parties for their officers and men in an effort to cheer them up. The women even put on a play, a 1712 Roman tragedy called "Cato," by English playwright Joseph Addison.

Every clear, cold morning, when bright sunshine glittered on the snow, Martha emerged from the Potts' house with a basket on her arm. Mrs. Westlake, a sixteen-year-old girl, strode beside her. When they entered each hut, the girl helped lift the men in her strong arms and spoon hot broth into their mouths. In the next cabin, an emaciated sergeant lay dying on a thin straw pallet. His young wife leaned over him. Martha had seen heartbreaking sights all day, but now tears threatened to fill her eyes. Gently, she fed him some of the food she had cooked. Then she knelt down by his low mattress and began to pray. Her sweet, serious tones filled the cabin. She prayed for the dying man who had given so much to his country and for the young wife who had come so far only to watch him die. Mrs. Westlake never forgot the experience.

Martha treating wounded soldiers (lower right).

Despite the sad sights she witnessed during her work, Martha continued to combine compassion with courage and determination. Sitting down at her desk at some moment during her busy day, she wrote, "I am still determined to be cheerful and happy, in whatever situation I may be; for I have also learned from experience that the greater part of our happiness or misery depends upon our dispositions, and not upon our circumstances." The soldiers found her motherly and gracious, "sweeten[ing] the cares of a hero and smooth[ing] the rugged pains of war." Pierre-Etienne Duponceau, a French volunteer soldier, watched Martha's daily rounds with admiration. "Her presence," he marveled, "inspired fortitude." When discouraged soldiers left from being with her, they came out "full of hope and confidence."

Each year that the Revolutionary War lasted, Martha managed to travel to the army's winter encampments where she stayed during the most difficult months. In the winter of 1775, she rode north to Cambridge, Massachusetts. When spring came, she trailed her husband and his army to New York. In the spring of 1777, she camped out at Washington's Morristown, New Jersey, headquarters. During the summer, she returned to Mount Vernon to supervise running the large plantation. This winter, she flew north like a contrary bird, to help shelter the men at Valley Forge. Again and again during the war, Martha Washington would stay at her husband's side throughout campaigns in New York, New Jersey, Maryland and Pennsylvania.

As Commander-in-Chief, Washington refused to accept any payment during the war. But later, Congress reimbursed George and Martha for their expenses for the war effort. Whenever Martha appeared in camp, the soldiers burst out shouting: "God bless Lady Washington!"

When General Baron von Steuben arrived to take command of drilling the soldiers, Washington called for a grand review parade. The camp at Valley Forge buzzed with excitement as soldiers who had survived the long winter cheered for the King of France and the Thirteen Colonies. But as the General and his wife appeared on the church steps after the morning service, the soldiers roared: "Long live Lady Washington!"

Through her compassion, Martha Washington had won a historical place in their hearts.

I am determined to be cheerful and happy in whatever situation I may find myself. For I have learned that the greater part of our misery or unhappiness is determined not by our circumstance but by our disposition.

—Martha Washington

Questions

1. In what ways did Martha Washington demonstrate compassion to the soldiers? to her husband?
2. Read Philippians 4:11 and compare what it says with what Lady Washington wrote about her determination.
3. What can we learn from Lady Washington about being an inspiration to others?
4. Think of someone you know who is going through hard times. What might you do to encourage them?
5. What are some of the functions Martha performed for the soldiers in camp?
6. Martha Washington used skills she had learned in managing Mount Vernon to bless others in need. What skills do you have that you might use to help others? Think of specific examples.

Orderliness

DEFINITION

Managing my life and my belongings in order to reach maximum potential

MEMORY VERSE

Let all things be done decently and in order.
1 Corinthians 14:40

The Drillmaster

Baron von Steuben

Valley Forge, Pennsylvania
February–March, 1778

Words failed him as he came to this dirty little valley huddled under the shadow of the Schuylkill Mountains. In the torchlight of a February evening, Baron Friedrich Wilhelm von Steuben stared at the huts and tents crowded together in the half-melted snow. Dead horses lay among the muddy muck, stripped of their meat, their bones gleaming. Soldiers with tangled hair, bloody feet, and ragged clothing hunched over small cooking fires, poking at the sticks with blackened bayonets. Not a single

Baron Friedrich Wilhelm von Steuben

man wore a proper uniform. Sickness hung over the black huts like mosquitoes over a swamp. He could see his work stretching ahead, long as the winter road that lay behind him. Some distance away, he caught sight of General George Washington's headquarters: a small stone house, belonging to the Quaker Isaac Potts, half-smothered in snow.

Stepping down from the carriage, Baron von Steuben introduced himself to the Commander-in-Chief of the Continental Army. Washington greeted him warmly. They had exchanged letters back and forth ever since Benjamin Franklin met the penniless, debt-ridden baron in Paris and realizing America's need for an effective military officer, recommended him to Congress. Arriving in December 1777, von Steuben immediately travelled south, seeking approval from Congress to serve as a volunteer without rank or pay. Congress, unable to believe their good fortune in securing a veteran of the Seven Years' War, and one who had served in the department of the quartermaster general

Suffering troops at Valley Forge

Baron von Steuben training troops to use bayonets

and as an aide-de-camp to Frederick the Great of Prussia, accepted his services and sent him on to Washington at Valley Forge.

Von Steuben's thick German accent bled through his letters to Washington. "The object of my greatest ambition," he insisted, "is to render your country all the service in my power, and to deserve the title of a citizen of America by fighting for the cause of your liberty. If the distinguished ranks in which I have served in Europe should be an obstacle, I had rather serve officers as have already distinguished themselves among you." He paused, adding: "I would say, moreover, were it not for the fear of offending your modesty, that your Excellency is the only person under whom, after having served under the King of Prussia, I could wish to pursue an art to which I have wholly given myself up."

No one could know that he was not a real baron. While his father had falsified his lineage in order to gain a better position at court, the Americans believed in the blue blood of this majestic, eccentric, and kindhearted Prussian officer. As the two tall men faced each other, possibly speaking in French, Washington asked von Steuben to act as Inspector General. As such, he would be responsible for training and disciplining the entire Continental Army. The baron wasted no time. Before the pale winter dawn spread over the camp, von Steuben finished buttoning his full-dress uniform with quick fingers. He drank his morning cup of coffee and leisurely smoked a pipe while his servant combed, fluffed, and tied his hair into a queue. As the first red rays of the sun struck across the mountain and fell on the snow, the baron swung himself onto his horse. The silver star of Prussian knighthood sparkled on his chest. While his staff officers, Ternan and Lieutenant Colonel Fleury, scrambled after him, von Steuben rode off to the parade ground alone.

What he saw horrified him. A straggling crowd of civilians stood waiting for him. No one wore regular uniforms. They did not understand military discipline. They slumped, spiritless, dejected, and shivering. He tried to get the men to learn how to march or load their weapons, but they blundered again and again. The baron shouted in broken English, and then in despair began yelling in French, German, and English. The men stared at him, uncomprehending. Shaking his head, the baron declared that a European army would have existed in this miserable condition for less than a month.

Von Steuben plunged into teaching the men the basics of tactics, discipline, and drill. To help him with his task, von Steuben created two ranks of inspectors under him. The lower would inspect brigades, while the higher would inspect several brigades. First, von Steuben selected one hundred twenty men to serve as a "model company" in his new military training program. He kept things simple, cutting the cumbersome motions in the manual of arms down to ten. As he instructed the men to reload their firearms, he abandoned four unnecessary motions, streamlining the process by reducing the number to fifteen. Early in the morning, dressed in full uniform, von Steuben strode out in front of his model company. As the men struggled to match their shuffling, uneven steps to the standard marching pace, von Steuben threw away the drum that ordinarily helped soldiers to keep time. Barking out his orders in German, and repeated loudly in English by Captain Walker, von Steuben showed them that they could march without a drum just by watching the rhythmic, swinging step of the officer at the head of the column.

Not only did American soldiers know nothing about marching in step, von Steuben found, but

Grand Parade of trained troops

his horror increased when he discovered that they had no idea how to use a bayonet, either. When Washington's men came out of winter quarters, they would face a powerful, well-trained British army skilled in the use of weaponry. When von Steuben entered camp, he saw men holding their bayonets over small fires to roast a piece of horseflesh, or using them as shovels to dig holes in the half-frozen ground. Von Steuben singlehandedly turned the bayonet from a cooking tool into a deadly fighting weapon. He made the men practice bayonet charges again and again, thrusting, parrying, and attacking.

Most of the Continental officers, von Steuben found, knew as little about manual exercises and drill as their men. As he drilled his model company, the baron found it difficult to explain exactly what he wanted since he could not tell them in plain English. When men stepped out of line, fumbled when loading a rifle, or blundered over an exercise, von Steuben could not tell them what to do. One day, he simply shouted and gesticulated in despair. Just then, Captain Benjamin Walker, an officer from a New York regiment, stepped forward and offered his help. The baron almost dropped with relief.

"Had I seen an angel from heaven," he exclaimed, "I could not have been more rejoiced."

Pleased at finally being understood, von Steuben made Captain Walker his aide-de-camp. From then on, he kept him at his side at all times. Now, whenever a soldier frustrated him, von Steuben yelled at his translator: "Over here! Yell at him for me!" Every day, the baron wrote out his next day's orders and handed them to Walker, who translated them into French. Then Fleury, his French-speaking officer, translated them into English for the benefit of the men.

For months, the men drilled faithfully throughout the camp. As soon as von Steuben's model company finished their course, he sent them out to train the other units, one after another, until the whole camp could perform drill. Instead of a huddled mass of cattle, the men now looked like soldiers, parading in single file with shouldered arms, the officers marching stiffly at the sides and in front. Now, the baron began lining the men up for inspection. Walking slowly along in front of them in his uniform and medals, von Steuben picked up one musket, tilted it to check on the soldier's cleaning and polishing job. Then he examined the men's accoutrements, such as their bullet pouch, gunpowder flask, and various belts, to make sure that they were organized and fastened properly. The men stood straight, their eyes quick, and their hands skilled with their weapons.

Von Steuben also worried about the Valley Forge camp's dirty, rundown condition. The soldiers had no latrines. Almost as soon as he arrived, the Baron swung into action. Instead of a hodgepodge clutter of huts and tents, he organized them into the standard camp layout that would last almost until the twentieth century. He created rows of tents that housed the general command, officers, and then enlisted men. He set up the kitchens at one end of camp, and built the latrines over on the opposite side, downhill from the camp. Once he had cleaned up the camp, Von Steuben went to work arranging each unit along company and regimental streets. The men had a chance to see the baron's kind heart in action when he went to the trouble to go over the doctors' reports, sat by the bedsides of sick men, and checked to make sure that everyone had warm lodgings, food, and clothing. These arrangements not only gave the men a better chance to survive the winter in a clean, organized environment, but the military formations also gave them a sense of discipline and identity with their unit. They were on the road to becoming a real fighting force instead of a mass of raw, patriotic farmers.

Their first baptism of fire under Von Steuben came at the Battle of Barren Hill on May 20, 1778. After only three months of training, Washington's men held their own against the British like never before. At the Battle of Monmouth on June 28, 1778, only von Steuben's training kept the men from being utterly defeated by superior British forces. His hard work paid off at the Battle of Stony Point when American soldiers, out of ammunition, ferociously

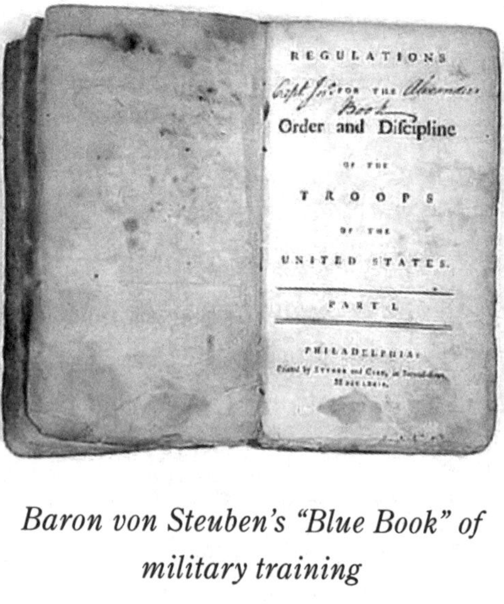

Baron von Steuben's "Blue Book" of military training

attacked the British troops with a bristling line of bayonets. The American victory at Stony Point proved that von Steuben's vital bayonet training was probably his greatest contribution to the American Revolution. During that winter, von Steuben began writing *Regulations for the Order and Discipline of the Troops of the United States.* Known as the "Blue Book," von Steuben's military training and administration system that he developed at Valley Forge would serve as the manual for the United States Army until the War of 1812.

Following the long winter at Valley Forge, the Marquis de Lafayette replaced the baron, who travelled south in April, 1781, to assist General Nathanael Greene in the southern campaign. While quartered in Virginia, von Steuben supplied the army with troops and supplies from a central supply dump. On September 13, he commanded one of Washington's three divisions as they advanced against Lord Cornwallis at Yorktown. When Cornwallis agreed to surrender on October 17th, von Steuben and his men crouched in the trenches that ringed the British position. In a final flourish of military etiquette, the baron kept his men in line until the British came out for the final surrender. Washington, in return for von Steuben's impressive work in training the army, wrote to Congress to give von Steuben the position of Inspector General. Having served for three years without thanks or pay, he would now receive military glory, and the rank and pay of a major general. Following the war, he settled down in America, his adopted homeland.

Baron von Steuben single-handedly transformed the Continental Army from a discouraged rabble into a well-trained army able to hold their own against the British. He demonstrated orderliness by training and organizing the men and adapting his tactics to the differences of the American army instead of sticking stubbornly to the European military model.

The object of my greatest ambition is to render your country all the service in my power, and to deserve the title of a citizen of America by fighting for the cause of your liberty.

—Baron Friedrich Wilhelm von Steuben

Questions

1. What was von Steuben's first impression of the Continental troops?
2. Who had recommended von Steuben's services to Congress?
3. What was von Steuben's experience in training troops?
4. What was von Steuben's motivation in assisting the Americans? Did he ask to be paid for his services?
5. What responsibilities did Washington give to von Steuben?
6. How did von Steuben establish order?
7. Who volunteered to aid von Steuben as interpreter?
8. How did von Steuben organize the camp?
9. How did the men see that von Steuben had a kind heart?
10. How did the men fare in their first Battle of Barren Hill? Battle of Monmouth?
11. How did the soldiers prove their good training at the Battle of Stony Point?

12. What proved to be von Steuben's greatest contribution to the American Revolution?
13. What was von Steuben's role at Yorktown?
14. What did von Steuben do following the war?
15. How can you benefit from practicing orderliness? What specific goal can you set to accomplish this?

Persistence

DEFINITION

Tenacity; strength to finish a task
despite adversity

MEMORY VERSE

Be ye strong therefore,
and let not your hands
be weak: for your work
shall be rewarded.
II Chronicles 15:7

March of the Long Knives

Col. George Rogers Clark

Vincennes, Missouri
May, 1778–February, 1779

They had marched towards the Ohio River for weeks now. Twenty-six-year-old Colonel George Rogers Clark watched as his men splashed across the Ohio near Fort Massac. His blue eyes scanned the woods near the river for danger. A forested wilderness stretched on either side. Birds whistled unseen in the foliage which masked the sounds of moving deer. Beyond the woods stretched the Illinois plains, rustling with hot grasses, and loud with the thunder of herds of buffalo. Clark knew that this region north of the Ohio River formed part of the Province of Quebec. Nothing existed here except bands of Indians, isolated little towns of French Creoles, and a few British garrisons at Detroit, Vincennes on the Wabash, and Kaskaskia and Cahokia on the Illinois River. British officers, accompanied by small detachments of regular troops, controlled these French outposts.

From his fort at Detroit, Lieutenant-Governor Major Henry Hamilton sent raiding parties out into the Ohio territory to harass settlers. Few settlers wanted to speculate in land or settle there with their families when threatened by attacks. In October, 1774, the raids and counter-raids escalated into Lord Dunmore's War, when Andrew Lewis and his Virginia militiamen won a bloody victory against the Shawnee at Point Pleasant. With this defeat, Virginia absorbed Kentucky into its state borders. At the same time, the embittered Native Americans had sided with the British during the Revolution. Major Hamilton, nicknamed the "Hair Buyer," encouraged the tribes' warriors to sweep down from the north, slaughtering American settlers for money. He paid them for each scalp that they brought in, ensuring British dominance over Ohio, Kentucky, and southern Illinois. The Virginia legislature realized that it needed to protect its settlers and territories. But the Continental Army, immersed in the war in New

Colonel George Rogers Clark

York, could not spare any men or resources to make a difference on the frontier.

Clark, a young surveyor, backwoods hunter, seasoned fighter, and militia officer stationed at Harrodsburg, Kentucky, took matters into his own

Clark's conference with the Creoles

hands. For some time, he had sent spies out into the Northwest Territory to gather intelligence on the British garrisons there. His information convinced Clark that once a small, select force of frontiersmen destroyed British influence with the Indians, they would be able to conquer the territory. In December 1777, he appealed to Governor Patrick Henry to authorize a secret expedition to the Ohio. Patrick Henry strongly approved the plan, and in December, the Virginia Assembly gave Clark the authority to raise a suitable force. He had found it difficult to find men willing to leave their families to fight in a wilderness far from home. In the end, Clark finally gathered one hundred fifty riflemen from the backwoods of Virginia and nicknamed them the "Long Knives."

In May 1778, they floated down the Ohio in flatboats, drifting and rowing by turns until they came to the roaring falls of the Ohio. There, in the forest, Clark stopped for a few days to build a log outpost at what is now the city of Louisville. While there, fifty or sixty men joined Clark's party, but a number of the volunteers soon deserted. With his force swelled to one hundred seventy-five dedicated riflemen, Clark went down to the boats and pushed off again downstream. They rowed in darkness, during a sudden eclipse of the sun.

Now, as he watched the tall, rugged woodsmen wade through the river in their rough hunting

The Long Knives crossing the Wabash

shirts and leather leggings, Clark knew that they were only a day's march from Kaskaskia. Slung across the crooks of their arms, the Long Knives carried long-barreled, small-bore rifles. They also toted five hundred pounds of gunpowder. Finally the little party landed at Fort Massac and began disembarking from the boats in order to march north to Kaskaskia on the Mississippi River, where the British commander of the entire territory had his headquarters. Approaching cautiously by night, Clark determined to avoid bloodshed by taking the British garrison, Creole militia, and their allies by surprise. Clark marched by night and hid by day. Finally, he reached the edge of the small village on the evening of July 4th. His men camped silently in the woods close by until night fell again.

Lights, music, and the sound of dancing flowed out of the small, square windows of the wooden stockade. Red-coated British officers threw a magnificent ball that night, inviting the black-haired Creole women to dance while almost all the villagers gathered to watch. As the music reached its height, Clark motioned to his men. Slipping softly through the darkness, they breached the town, pouncing on the sentries, and circling the fort without a sound. Every able-bodied British soldier had gone inside the fort to dance or watch the merrymaking.

Posting his men around the fort in the warm summer darkness, Clark turned and walked confidently right through the open door into the fort. For a few moments, the slim young Colonel leaned against the wall, watching as men and women spun in the flaring red torchlight and light glinting off the officers' swords. In the heat and confusion, no one noticed him. Just then, a Native American man lying on the ground with his chin cupped in his hand glanced over at the stranger leaning against the wall. Suddenly, he leapt to his feet, letting loose a war-whoop that tore through the room. The dancers froze, and men bumped and jostled against each other in a terrified melee. Pushing himself away from the wall, Clark informed the Creoles they had nothing to fear. From now on, they would dance under the flag of the United States instead of the banner of Great Britain. Stunned into submission, not a single Frenchman resisted the Long Knives.

For the next twenty-four hours, the Creoles remained in uncertain anxiety about their fate. Finally, Clark called their leaders to a conference, explaining that he wanted to be their ally. If they joined his force, they would be treated with equal respect as American citizens. The Creoles gratefully accepted Clark's conditions. A local French priest offered to go to Vincennes as a messenger and persuade the French townspeople to change their allegiance from the British crown and surrender to the American flag.

Leaving the fort and his new Creole allies, Clark marched on Cahokia near modern-day St. Louis and captured it easily. With reinforcements running low, Clark decided to hold back until he could receive more men from Williamsburg. At the same time, Major Hamilton, the "Hair Buyer," caught wind of Clark's dangerous activities in the Ohio Territory and determined to stop him. Hamilton charged out of Detroit at the head of a small group of British regulars. Traveling south during October, he gathered

Loyalists, partisans, and Native American warriors, swelling his force to a terrifying five hundred men. He floated downriver with a vast flotilla of canoes rowed by armed troops. When the Creoles learned of Hamilton's approach, they refused to fight the formidable British governor known for his fondness of gathering scalps. The lone American officer, sent by Clark to Vincennes, had no choice except to surrender on December 17th.

Feeling easy in his mind, Hamilton decided to settle in for the winter. With snow coming on, making marching difficult if not impossible, he chose not to confront Clark in spite of the fact that he outnumbered Clark three-to-one. Instead, he dismissed all his Native American allies and sent some of his troops back to Detroit. In the spring, Hamilton announced, he would destroy Clark. If Clark had waited for the snow to melt, he would doubtless have been defeated by Hamilton's superior force. But he did something that Hamilton never dreamed he would do.

Discovering that Hamilton had sent away all his allies and many of his troops, the Colonel decided not to wait until the snow melted. He knew that his only hope lay in striking before Hamilton reassembled his troops again in the spring. Gathering his Long Knives and a handful of Creole volunteers, Clark and his shrunken party of one hundred thirty men started out on the long trail to Vincennes. But no roads existed in this trackless country. At first, they ploughed across the rolling, snow-covered Illinois prairies, broken only by vast dark patches of woods. In spite of their hardships, the men never went hungry. Shots rang out from the line, bringing a deer, elk, or buffalo crashing to the ground. At night, they broiled the meat over huge bonfires, feasting. Satisfied, they wrapped themselves in their coats and blankets and lay down by the embers to sleep.

In mid-February, they reached the flooded lands of the Wabash. Ice broke up in the river, drowning the bleak countryside as far as the eye could see. Day after day, Clark's men waded through icy water that soaked through their clothes and chilled their bones. Each step grew more painful and impossible. At night, they searched through the darkness for a small hillock where they could drag their wet, cold, and exhausted bodies above the water to sleep. During this bitter time, only Clark's personal courage and persistence kept them going. Finally, on February 23rd, after marching more than one hundred eighty miles through flooded plains and forests, Clark's men caught sight of Vincennes. Out in the woods they captured a Creole who had gone out to shoot ducks. The man told them that no one, not even the Native Americans in town, suspected their presence.

Major Hamilton surrenders to Colonel Clark

Clark debated what to do. The British regulars, headed by Major Hamilton, occupied a small fort at one end of the village. Two light guns protruded from the loopholes. Clark worried that if he suddenly attacked the town at night, the inhabitants would fight him out of terror. Clark needed them on his side, or to at least remain neutral. He decided to send the Creole duck hunter back in to warn the townspeople that an attack was imminent. But, he assured them, he only wanted to defeat the British. If everyone stayed quiet in their homes during the attack, no one would touch them. The duck hunter went in as planned, but his news surprised the Creoles, who jabbered about it anxiously, not certain what to do. In the end, the Native Americans, fearing a large force, hid in the nearby woods while the Creoles shut themselves up in their houses. The British knew nothing until Clark entered the village streets after nightfall. Rushing to the end of the street, Clark's Long Knives surrounded the fort and trapped the British inside.

The next morning, a war party returned from raiding the settlements in Kentucky on Hamilton's orders. They suddenly found themselves surrounded by furious frontiersmen. Giving no quarter for those who had shown no mercy to women and children, Clark killed the Native American prisoners in front of the fort while the British looked on.

Still, Hamilton stubbornly refused to surrender, although he believed that Clark possessed a numerically superior force. The battle continued desultorily during the next few days. The Redcoats fought hard, defending themselves skillfully. But Clark's keen-eyed sharpshooters picked off every gunner that appeared at a loophole with their long rifles. Finally, with British guns disabled and most of his men dead, Hamilton caved in and surrendered. Clark placed the men under guard, sending the notorious "Hair Buyer" and his troops to jail in Williamsburg. In the victory's aftermath, Clark renamed the outpost Fort Patrick Henry.

After his successful victory at Vincennes, Clark and his men patrolled the west for the next several years, solidifying Virginia's right to the territory. The British never again made an attempt to harass American settlers there. Following the Treaty of Paris in 1783, the Old Northwest became the heart of the United States of America. If Clark had not conquered this territory during the Revolution, it would have remained part of the British Dominion of Canada.

When George Washington learned about Clark's celebrated victory, he used it as leverage to ally the American colonies with France. Clark had conquered the Old Northwest Territory without any funds or assistance from the regular Continental Army. Taking advantage of the situation, Virginia claimed the entire new Territory, renaming it Illinois County. The vast state of Virginia now extended from Kentucky all the way to Wisconsin.

George Rogers Clark demonstrated persistence with each step of his plan to defeat the British in Ohio. In doing so, he was able to avoid unnecessary bloodshed and gain a victory important to the war on the American frontier.

Questions

1. What did Major Henry Hamilton entice the Native Americans to do? What was his nickname?
2. How did Clark demonstrate initiative in coming up with a plan?
3. Tell of the obstacle Clark and his men met up with and the persistence they employed to overcome it.
4. How did they overpower the fort of Creoles?
5. What did Clark do when he heard that Hamilton had sent away all his allies?
6. Tell of the men's persistence in wading through icy waters and other obstacles to accomplish their goal.
7. Tell what happened at the Battle of Vincennes.
8. What was a result of the victory at Vincennes?
9. What task awaits you that you could apply persistence to accomplish?
10. Think of a person in real life who demonstrates persistence to you.

Bravery

DEFINITION

To face danger without fear

MEMORY VERSE

Fear thou not; for I am with thee:
be not dismayed; for I am thy God:
I will strengthen thee; yea, I will help thee;
yea, I will uphold thee with the right hand
of my righteousness.

Isaiah 41:10

We Shall Not Fight Without Our Flag

Sgt. William Jasper

Sullivan's Island, South Carolina/Savannah, Georgia
June 28, 1776 and October 9, 1779

British warships appeared on the horizon of the island before the defenders had finished the fort. Scrambling onto the parapets, the American soldiers peered across the brilliant, hot sand towards the blue harbor. The ships anchored out in the bay and disgorged thousands of redcoats. Slowly, the stationary deck guns aboard the warships aimed towards the half-finished palmetto fort. It stood open to attack, one side and its entire back gaping wide. Twenty-nine-year-old Sergeant William Jasper, crouched over his gun battery, watched

British attack on Sullivan's Island, South Carolina

as the blue-and-crescent-moon flag, personally designed by Colonel William Moultrie, ran proudly up the pole, fluttering faintly in the heavy air. Known as a "genial, drawling" soldier, Jasper knew that if the British took Fort Sullivan, they would then take Charles Towne. With Charles Towne in British hands, Lord Cornwallis could penetrate the South Carolina interior and win the campaign in the South.

As the warships closed in, turning their two hundred seventy-one siege guns on the fort, and shells thudded against walls, Jasper thought briefly of Elizabeth. Just thinking about her thrust him back to that dark, cold autumn day in 1767 when he stepped off the immigrant boat, the *Minerva,* at Philadelphia and into a new world. He was only sixteen. He knew no one. His bewildered tongue could only wrap itself around German words. He stared up at shop signs that he could not have understood even if he spoke English, because he could neither read nor write. Hustled along the chilly streets, he arrived at an immigrant building. There, he gulped down warm soup, and then moved into a line to take the oath of allegiance and sign his name. Jasper stared at the paper. He had no idea what to put down, so he scratched an X, looking up to mutter his name, "Johann Wilhelm Gasper," to a bored-looking immigration official. The man quickly anglicized his name, scribbled "John William Jasper" on the sheet, and waved him on.

A heavy shell crashed into the fort, raining a shower of earth and splinters down on his head. Jasper strained his muscles, working with his gun crew, shoving a shell into the chamber, and directing the shot towards a British ship close by. Elizabeth. He had met his sweetheart while working a menial job as an indentured servant. He knew that he wanted to stay with her forever. When he finished his eight years as an indentured servant, he left Pennsylvania and travelled south to this sunny land of swamps and palmetto leaves to look for land. On July 7, 1775, he enlisted as a private in the 2nd South Carolina Regiment, one of six units raised across the colony when the Continental Congress called for troops following the battles of Lexington and Concord. Despite the poor pay, he hoped to earn enough to buy a plot of land. After two or three years, he scraped together enough money to purchase and clear his own spot of land in Georgia colony. He would never forget the day that he finally sent for Elizabeth, and she arrived, ready to set up housekeeping on his little farm. He had known then that he could not live without her. They married a short time later. In the twelve years since he came to America from Germany, he had forgotten what it meant to have another homeland. He would fight for this soil that had given him home and freedom till his last breath.

The hot sun beat down on his head and smoke streaked his face. Explosions rang in his ears. Despite the gunfire, dust, and heat, Jasper carried out his orders coolly and eagerly. Several days before, he and his fellow Continentals had been ordered to disembark at Sullivan's Island, a strategic post for the defense of Charles Towne Harbor against the British navy. When they arrived on a sweltering June day, Jasper reported to Colonel William Moultrie, who hurried around the site, supervising the defense of the harbor. While technically not the ranking officer on the island, Moultrie had practical control of the operation, since General Charles Lee

Colonel William Moultrie

had received strict orders to simply "observe" the assignment. Colonel Moultrie knew that the British could appear at any moment. Several days before their ships appeared on the horizon, the colonel began building a fort to defend the harbor from attack. American officers set off in the direction of the local plantations, hidden in dense palmetto thickets conscripting free men and slaves to help build the fort. Sweating under the hot South Carolina sun, soldiers, slaves, and local men began chopping down the tough palmettos and knocking them together to raise the walls and defense positions.

The British arrived before they had completed the fort. A ten-hour siege began as the defenders struggled against superior forces. As the afternoon wore on, Jasper and the other gun crews ran dangerously low on ammunition. They began to reserve their shot, firing only when the warships circled closer around the fort. Suddenly, a British shell crashed into the blue-and-white-crescent flag, shattering the pole. The colors toppled into the bottom of the ditch outside the fort wall. In the distance, South Carolina citizens watching anxiously from the roofs in Charles Towne knew that their men still held the harbor against the British. When the flag disappeared, their hearts sank.

Jasper saw the flag fall amid the smoke. "Colonel, don't let us fight without our flag!" he shouted.

Colonel Moultrie turned. "How can you help it?" he demanded. "The staff is gone."

Jasper did not say another word. Without thinking, he rose from his protected position, leaped across an embrasure and down into the ditch, straight into the face of heavy enemy fire. Running along the full length of the fort, he found the flag lying on the hot sand. Cutting the flag away from the pole, he lifted it in his arms and scrambled back up over the wall. Shouting for a sponge-staff from a nearby gun, Jasper tied the colors onto the staff. Then he climbed to the top of the parapet and rammed it into the wall facing the British. Facing the blazing ships, he let loose three cheers. Then he sprang down and returned to firing his gun.

Jasper's brave act rallied the American troops, giving them the strength to hold out until sunset stained the western sky. As the sun went down in a red ball of fire, the British suddenly boarded

Sergeant Jasper raises the flag at Fort Sullivan

their ships and retreated from Sullivan Island. They would not conquer Charles Towne until several years later. Later, the South Carolinians renamed the fortification Fort Moultrie.

Seige of Savannah, Georgia

Impressed by Jasper's bravery, Susannah Elliot, the wife of Jasper's captain, presented him with two silk flags. Governor John Rutledge presented his own sword to the sergeant at a military review held shortly after the battle. When the Governor also offered him a lieutenant's commission, Jasper politely turned it down, explaining that he would only be an embarrassment since he could not read or write. Instead, he accepted a "roving commission" from Colonel Moultrie to act as an American scout. Brave, active, a master of disguise, and a "very great partisan," the young sergeant not only recaptured American prisoners from British hands but also made several trips behind enemy lines, bringing back vital information.

On September 8, 1779, twenty-two French warships accompanied by ten troopships unloaded 4,000 soldiers at Tybee Island to help the patriots dislodge the British from Savannah. More than six hundred Continental soldiers and three hundred fifty militiamen, led by General Benjamin Lincoln, marched through the yellowing leaves of a southern autumn to join the French. British General Augustin Prevost, leading 1800 British forces, was entrenched in the Spring Hill fort at Savannah. The month-long siege dragged on into October.

Finally, on October 9th, General Lincoln determined to break the stalemate. He hurled his colonials and 3500 French soldiers at the walls of the fort. Gunfire blazed over the parapets, massacring four hundred Americans and six hundred Frenchmen. Mangled bodies littered the defense position and the ditch outside soon filled up with piles of dead men in colonial and French uniforms. Sheltered by the fort above, the British lost only about one hundred fifty men. In the thick of the fight, Sergeant Jasper looked up and saw the blue flag emblazoned with a crescent moon and the words Liberty tumble to the ground, held by a dying officer, Lieutenant Bush, from the 2nd Regiment. Seizing the fallen colors from the dead man's hand, Jasper struggled upwards to the fort to plant the American colors on the parapet as he had at Fort Moultrie. Suddenly, a bullet struck his body. The young man crumpled into the bloody ditch, the colors wrapped around his body, and his hand still gripping the flag. He had made his last stand. He was twenty-nine years old.

Minutes later, the enemy breached the line, shoving the Americans back. As the 2nd South Carolina retreated, they carried away the other silk flag. Later, British soldiers, picking over the dead bodies, tore the flag that Jasper had tried to save out of his cold hand. They shipped it off to London, where the King's Royal Rifles proudly displayed it in their trophy room. Sergeant William Jasper was buried hastily, in an unmarked grave in the raw earth at Spring Hill Fort, along with hundreds of his comrades.

Several days after the brutal attack and repulse, the French sailed away in their warships, abandoning Savannah to the British. Despite Lincoln's failure to take Savannah, the story of Jasper's bravery became well known through the budding republic.

Today, Jasper County in Georgia is named after him, as well as the Jasper Spring State Historical Marker in Savannah, Georgia. A fifteen-foot bronze statue of Sergeant Jasper, sculpted in 1888 by Alexander Doyle, stands in the center of Madison Square, gazing out on the harbor that he once tried to defend. With the blue flag thrown over his shoulder and a sword in his hand, Jasper seems to be repeating the words that are carved beneath him: "We shall not fight without our flag."

Although he is little remembered today, Sergeant William Jasper became an important figure in early American history. Jasper demonstrated bravery by twice rescuing his regimental colors from the British and inspiring his fellow soldiers to victory at Fort Moultrie.

Sergeant Jasper was one of the purest patriots and bravest men that the Revolution produced. His heroism was of the quiet, unostentatious kind, springing from duty and devotion, not from the thirst of fame.

—Benson J. Lossing
Pictorial Field Book of the Revolution
(1850)

Questions

1. Why was it crucial to prevent the British from taking Fort Sullivan?
2. Tell about John Jasper coming to this country.
3. When did he move to South Carolina?
4. Why was he passionate about protecting his freedom?
5. How did Moultrie's men prepare for the coming attack?
6. What did Jasper do when he saw the flag fall?
7. How did his brave act affect the troops?
8. How was he later rewarded for his bravery?
9. What happened when the patriots tried to dislodge the British from Savannah?
10. Again Jasper witnessed the flag fall. What did he do this time?
11. How old was Jasper when he gave his life for his country?
12. How did Jasper's bravery inspire the other soldiers?

Creativity

DEFINITION

Seeking godly wisdom for a new way
to get the job done

MEMORY VERSE

And be not conformed to this world:
but be ye transformed by the renewing of
your mind, that ye may prove what is
that good, and acceptable,
and perfect, will of God.

Romans 12:2

The Fighting Chaplain

Rev. James Caldwell

Springfield, New Jersey
c. June 19, 1780

This was a year of fire and blood. The War for Independence, now entering its fifth year, tottered on the brink of defeat. More than six hundred men had deserted Washington's ragged army at Morristown, New Jersey. Paper currency floated as worthless as ashes in the wind. Charleston, South Carolina, had fallen to General Cornwallis. Creeping out from the starved and disease-ridden winter at Valley Forge, the Continental Army now faced a new invasion that tore into the countryside.

Rev. James Caldwell

British General Sir Henry Clinton and Baron Wilhelm von Knyphausen had landed a massive invasion force from Staten Island on the New Jersey shore. The British intended to strike a death-blow that would end the American Revolution. The Hessians came down like a cloud of locusts. For two weeks, they covered the green fields between Elizabethtown and Connecticut Farms. Setting fire to the wooden houses, they retreated and pushed the Americans back towards Springfield.

Suddenly, rounding the turnpike, they ran straight into American Colonel Israel Angell and his handful of soldiers hunkering down in an apple orchard opposite the Rahway River. Forty-six-year-old Reverend James Caldwell watched as the Redcoats opened fire with a murderous volley. Musket balls slashed the branches overhead, sending deadly spears of wood flying through the air. Dubbed the "Fighting Chaplain," he had appeared in his pulpit the Sunday after independence from England was declared in 1776 and slammed two loaded pistols down beside his Bible. Since that day, he preached and gathered supplies for the beleaguered American Army. Now, he marched up and down the line of soldiers, encouraging them.

Five thousand Hessians faced them across the valley, outnumbering them five-to-one. Six artillery pieces blasted into their thin ranks, killing their single artillery gunner. As the losses mounted, Colonel Angell continued to hold off the superior force almost by sheer willpower. But Caldwell knew that they could not hold out much longer. Suddenly, the soldiers ran out of wadding with which to pack their bullets. No wadding, no shooting! There was a time for prayers and a time for action. That time had come. He knew what he had to do.

Seizing his horse, he leaped astride it. His fair hair blowing around his face, he galloped through the town like Paul Revere. In his own lifetime, he too, had seen the horror of clashing ideologies and beliefs. Britain and America could not peacefully coexist until these worldviews had been reconciled. The reconciliation had come only through blood, and he still hoped for it, even in these dark days as the revolution shuddered on its foundation and Knyphausen's men pressed closer.

Swinging down from his horse, he dashed into the dim church. Glaring around, he grabbed stacks of hymnals, filling his arms with them. Smoke blew around his face as he ran down the steps to his horse. He could see his wife Hannah's face smiling at him through the smoke of the battle, the baby in her arms and his three-year-old clinging to her dress. Two weeks ago, Knyphausen had landed, bringing his Hessians swarming across the land. They burned his Presbyterian church, along with irreplaceable records and sermons. Near Springfield, Caldwell saw smoke mushroom suddenly on the horizon. He could hear his own cry: "Thank God! The fire is not in the direction of my house." But he had been wrong. As he came closer, he could see his house burning and he knew that this was the end, the end of everything he had hoped and dreamed. He galloped up on horseback, amid smoke and flames. His wife was lying on the ground outside their home, her clothes torn. A Hessian soldier had shot her twice through the window as she huddled on the bed with her children. Then they had torn open her clothes and pockets to find the few silver items she had frantically hidden on her body as she tried to protect the children. "They will respect a mother," she said over and over. But they had not. He had tried to move them to a safer place in town, but Hannah, not wanting to move on the open road with young children, had stayed behind. She would always be with him, although she was gone, as she had left him that day.

Rev. Caldwell giving hymnals to use as ammunition

Now, his calm face changed, fired with grief, passion, and energy. It was as if he had shed an old coat with the fight. His voice burst over the screams and shots, so powerful that the men heard him over the shrill notes of the fife and the pounding of the drums and turned. Splinters from the apple trees whizzed overhead as James Caldwell galloped up on horseback, throwing out handfuls of hymnals, full of the hymns of Isaac Watts, to the patriots on either side.

"Give 'em Watts, Boys!" he shouted. "Give 'em Watts!"

Wheeling on the Hessians, the Continental soldiers poured lead into their ranks. The British ultimately drove the Americans from Springfield, but the moral boost and physical aid given by Caldwell's creativity helped the colonists to hold out much longer than they could otherwise have done.

Give 'em Watts, boys–give 'em Watts!

—Reverend James Caldwell

Questions

1. What had recently happened to Reverend Caldwell's wife?
2. How did the British intend to strike a death-blow that would end the American Revolution?
3. How badly did the Hessians outnumber the Americans?
4. What catastrophe befell the Americans?
5. How did Reverend Caldwell overcome the problem by using creativity?
6. What did he say as he distributed the hymnals to the men?
7. Think of a tough situation you face. How could you use creativity to make it better?

Alertness

DEFINITION

Being keenly aware of what is taking place around me so I can be prepared with a right response

MEMORY VERSE

Watch ye and pray, lest ye enter into temptation. The spirit truly is ready, but the flesh is weak.

Mark 14:38

Road to Perdition

John Paulding & Companions

New York

September, 1780

Glancing over his shoulder, the young British officer, wearing his crimson and white regimental coat, entered Joshua Hett Smith's house on the western bank of the Hudson River. Inside, General George Clinton's spy-in-chief Major John Andre shook hands with the heavy-jowled man with whom he had been secretly corresponding for over a year: Benedict Arnold. Speaking quietly, the men discussed the final plans for selling West Point out to the British. Down at Verplanck's Point, American

Colonel James Livingston Smith opened fire on the *HMS Vulture,* the sloop-of-war that had carried Andre to meet Arnold.

Benedict Arnold

Looking out the window, Andre saw that the boat, badly damaged, had retreated downriver, leaving him stranded on the American side. At this, Arnold forced Andre to take off his British uniform and put on a civilian coat so that, if caught, he would not get into trouble. Smith, who often spied for both sides, expressed surprise that Andre, supposedly acting on civilian business from New York, was dressed in a British uniform. Andre, smiling a little at his own vanity, said that he had borrowed the coat from a military friend for the occasion. Smith offered him one of his own coats. Andre wrapped himself in the worn, dark greatcoat, the wide cape fluttering over his shoulders, and buttoned it close to his slender neck. Meanwhile, Arnold scribbled out passes that would let Andre safely through the lines.

An orange sunset spread across the evening sky as Andre, accompanied by Smith and his servant, rode off towards King's Ferry, intending to take the overland route back to New York. Arnold, watching them as they rode out of sight, knew that he had reached the last stage in his plans to turn West Point with its supplies over to the British.

It was hard to say when he first started on the road to perdition. In 1778, thirty-seven-year-old widower Benedict Arnold, a prominent member of the Philadelphia social scene after his expedition to British-held Quebec, Canada, walked into beautiful, lively, eighteen-year-old Peggy Shippen's parlor. The daughter of Judge Edward Shippen, a Loyalist sympathizer, Peggy lived at the center of social life in the city. Some whispered that the handsome young British officer, Major John Andre, had courted her after his imprisonment by American troops. Within a year, Benedict Arnold won and married Peggy Shippen, and threw himself into an extravagant whirl of parties, entertainment, and intrigue. After helping to capture Fort Ticonderoga and leading the Quebec campaign, Arnold felt neglected by Congress. They had not given him the rank, appreciation, or funds that he felt he deserved for risking his life and health for the American cause.

Appointed as the military commander of Philadelphia, Arnold's dissatisfaction and extravagant spending continued. Congress, suspicious that Arnold had begun engaging in "illegal and oppressive acts," called for a court-martial to investigate the matter. In January 1780, the court-martial cleared him of all charges except on one or two minor counts, but ordered Arnold to pay reparations amounting to one thousand pounds for unaccounted expenditures during his Quebec campaign. Nursing his bitterness, discontent, and growing disillusionment with the American cause, Arnold resigned from the army.

During the war, Peggy and her social circle had ways of keeping in touch with lovers across enemy lines in spite of military orders that banned communication with the foe. Peggy introduced her husband to her old suitor, Major Andre, who had just been named British spy-in-chief for General George Clinton the previous year.

Another intermediary, a man named Stansbury, served as courier for the secret communication opened between Arnold and Clinton. Andre worked as the intermediary. They disguised the letters, written in cipher and invisible ink, as mercantile correspondence and delivered them through Peggy's women's circle for safety. Only Peggy knew that certain letters contained instructions from General Clinton. Arnold, calling himself "Gustavus"

Peggy Shippen, Mrs. Benedict Arnold

The Smith House

and Andre "John Anderson," made it clear that he wanted to hurt the American cause and contribute to British victory as much as possible. At the same time, he wanted a substantial monetary reward in return for his services. John Brown, a lower-ranking American officer, wrote of Arnold: "Money is this man's God, and to get enough of it, he would sacrifice his country."

To this end, Arnold wrote to Washington, asking for the command at West Point. West Point, near the Hudson River, possessed both a strategic location and large stores of military supplies. Interested in Arnold's offer, Clinton ordered Andre to discover what kind of intelligence the American could actually provide them. Even prior to his court-martial, Arnold passed information about troop numbers, movements, and supply depots on to the British. Clinton began pressing for a face-to-face meeting with his agent around the same time that he captured Stony Point, New York, sending Washington's army tumbling in retreat.

Arnold, now in command at West Point, worried that the British no longer trusted him. He wrote again to Clinton in August, 1780, offering to sell out West Point for £20,000 pounds with a down-payment of £1,000 pounds. On August 15, Andre sent him Clinton's final offer. He would give Arnold the £20,000 pounds without indemnity. Arnold at West Point now controlled the entire American side of the Hudson River all the way from Albany to the British lines near New York City. He immediately began weakening West Point's defenses, cutting down on military strength, and selling off the supply stores so as to make a siege more likely to succeed. At the same time, he wrote to Andre to accept Clinton's offer. Four days later, he fired off a ciphered letter to New York, carried by the wife of a war prisoner. Clinton felt that his agent and the American traitor ought to meet.

The two men set the date for September 11th near Dobb's Ferry. But British gunboats, lying off-shore and unaware of Arnold's arrival, fired at his boat. Forced to retire, the men finally met at Smith's house on September 21. When Colonel James Livingston fired on the *HMS Vulture,* Andre could no longer go back by the Hudson. Accompanied by Smith, he set off over a dangerous overland route, hoping that Arnold's passports would protect him.

Capture of Major Andre

On the way from Stony Point to Verplanck's Point, Smith chattered incessantly, trying to get the young officer to talk on one subject or another. He racked his brains for something to interest him. But Andre kept very quiet, his face sad and thoughtful. He spoke briefly, only answering when asked a question. Near the ferry, they came upon a group of loungers whom Smith knew. Smith, perhaps trying to divert suspicion, lingered with them, joking, laughing, and drinking a bowl of punch near a sutler's tent. Meanwhile, Andre, saying nothing, slowly walked his horse along the river bank. He waited near the ferry as Smith hurried up. Across the river, an hour later, they ran into an American patrol party headed by a Captain Boyd. Boyd asked them so many questions, particularly what "important business" had brought them into the wilderness at night, that Andre began to feel nervous. Boyd warned them that the British "cowboys" were out below them. The "cowboys" were Loyalists for the British that attacked Patriots and stole cattle for British Forces. They should think twice about going on until morning.

In order to avoid raising suspicion, Andre and Smith stopped at Andreas Miller's house nearby to sleep for the night. Inside the house, they found cramped living quarters but a warm welcome. Forced to sleep in the same bed with Smith because of the lack of space, the slight British officer lay down, but not to sleep. Exhausted, but too tense to close his eyes, Andre tossed and turned beside his rough companion. Heavy thoughts weighed on his mind. Nearby, Captain Boyd and his troopers kept an uneasy eye out for the British cowboys.

Dawn broke. Andre stirred, cold and weary, while Smith shook his servant awake. The horses stood saddled at the door, ready for an early departure. Andreas Miller shook his head, refusing to take any money for his hospitality. The two men mounted their horses and rode through the cool morning air along the road towards Pine's Bridge. Andre's troubled face brightened a little as they put distance between them and Boyd's patrolling party. Suddenly, he began talking pleasantly and cheerfully on a great variety of subjects. Now and then, Smith glanced at Andre, astonished at the change. No longer silent and gloomy, the young officer discussed poetry, literature, and the arts. Sometimes, he spoke of the war, how it grieved him, and his hope for a quick peace.

Riding along in this way, they saw no one until they came within two and a half miles of Pine's Bridge. All at once, Smith stopped his horse. He would go no further. Trembling, he insisted that the British cowboys lurked in the neutral area between the two armies. Some had even seen the Skinners, bloodthirsty raiders who claimed to ride on the American side. As a double spy, he could not risk being captured by either side. Saying goodbye, Smith turned and galloped towards home. As he left, he had no idea of the identity of the man with whom he had just spent a pleasant hour discussing cultured ideas.

Andre wheeled his horse and faced the dangerous country, a wilderness thirty miles wide, crisscrossed by bands of cutthroats and murderers little interested in the war except for their ability to skim profit off either side. As Smith's dust dwindled in the distance, Andre slipped off the road to White

Plains and instead turned towards Tarrytown. If he could meet up with the British cowboys, he knew that he would be safe. It was now between nine and ten o'clock on Saturday morning, September 23rd.

He could not know that seven young American soldiers had set up an ambush on this same road, half a mile from the village at Tarrytown. Some days, they caught suspicious people and shook them down for money. Other days, they managed to capture droves of cattle that a lone boy might be driving along the road towards the markets in New York. Bored with the long wait, three of them, John Paulding, David Williams, and Isaac Van Wart, crouched in the bushes at the edge of the road. Andre rode along, submersed in his thoughts. He had not seen a single soul since leaving White Plains. Nearing the bank of the Hudson River, he rode over a little brook that dipped down in the road. Hills rose on either side. Tangled trees and autumn undergrowth darkened the sky.

Suddenly, one of the young men sat up and whispered to Paulding, "There comes a gentlemanlike-looking man, who appears to be well dressed, and has boots on, and whom you had better step out and stop, if you don't know him." They particularly noticed that he wore fine boots—a precious commodity in that time and place.

Paulding, wearing a green Hessian coat with red trim, reared up at Andre, shoving his musket at the officer's chest. The others, bursting out of the thicket to the west of the road, ordered him to stand still. Andre stared at them, his face a little pale but still calm.

"Gentlemen," he said quietly, "I hope you belong to our party."

Paulding retorted, "What party?"

Andre said quickly: "The Lower Party."

Paulding cautiously agreed that he did.

Then Andre did not attempt to pretend. "I am a British officer out of the country on particular business," he said pleasantly, "and I hope you will not detain me a minute."

To convince them that he really was a British officer, he pulled his engraved watch out of his worn coat.

Instead, Paulding roughly ordered him to dismount.

The young officer suddenly seemed to realize his danger. He exclaimed, "I must do anything to get along."

He gave a strangled laugh and pulled out General Arnold's pass. The men squinted at it. They would discover that, made out to John Anderson, it allowed him to pass through the guards to the region below White Plains. Andre submitted to dismounting, but protested: "Gentlemen, you had best let me go, or you will bring yourselves into trouble, for your stopping me will detain the general's business." He explained that he was on his way to Dobb's Ferry to meet a man there to obtain military intelligence for Arnold.

The Fidelity Medallion presented to John Paulding, David Williams, and Isaac Van Wart

Looking at Andre suspiciously, Paulding continued: "There are many bad people, who are going along the road, and I do not know but perhaps he might be one."

Andre waited. Then Paulding shook his head. A British officer in civilian clothes was undoubtedly a spy. He might have let Andre go, he later argued, but Andre had already told him honestly that he was a British officer and they could not let a British officer escape. It seemed that Andre could not win either as a British officer or a civilian spy. Either way, he was doomed.

Guns in hand, the men herded Andre into the bushes. There, they ordered him to take off his clothes while they searched him carefully for secret correspondence. They found nothing. They found no money either. They would not forget the elegant, gentlemanly clothing that he wore, the clothing that shone like jewels in the dark wood and first convinced them to stop him. Andre silently laid aside his blue caped overcoat. Underneath, he wore a slim-fitting frock coat that shone like red claret wine, the buttonholes laced with glittering gold tinsel. Even the buttonholes, the men noticed, were stitched with gold lace. Wearing a round tri-corn hat, light nankeen waistcoat and knee breeches, Andre must have seemed to them to have stepped out of another world — a brief flash of candlelight and crystal, powdered hair, women's laughter, and soft music — the world of art, poetry, and literature that he had, with a sad kind of gaiety, spoken of an hour before. All the things they had lost by the war.

Andre, shivering in the autumn air, had apparently forgotten to remove his boots. Andre had given them no presents, such as they usually obtained one way or another from passing travelers. They shook one boot and found it empty. Then they heard a crackle in Andre's thread stockings and pounced, forcing him to pull them off. Standing barefoot, Andre watched as they seized the wad of papers he had carefully placed in his stocking under his foot. Paulding had no doubts now. A spy, he hissed. Eagerly, they stripped off his other boot and stocking and found three more papers hidden there.

Roughly, they ordered Andre to dress himself. Then Paulding asked if Andre would give them any amount of money that they asked for. The officer agreed.

"Would you give us your horse, saddle, bridle, watch, and 100 guineas?" he pressed.

Andre said, "Yes."

He offered to give them as much dry goods or any amount of money that they pleased. He would then bring it to the place that they named so that they could pick the money up. Since he carried no money on him, Paulding suspected that Andre might not be able to get that much money together.

"No," he snapped, "if you would give us ten thousand guineas, you would not stir a step." The words had a nice, patriotic ring. Besides, they would later echo heroically in court after he collected his medal and his reward, and after he had forgotten Andre's face.

Paulding demanded to know if Andre would try to escape if he could.

Honestly and as an officer, Andre replied, "Yes, I would."

His agreement came as no surprise. Paulding and his friends would have done the same thing if captured. Paulding growled that he would not let him get away. Hurrying Andre along, they badgered him with questions. Stopping under a shady tree, the officer begged them to stop asking questions. He would remain silent until he saw their commander-in-chief. Then he would tell him everything.

The three men escorted him to the nearest military outpost at North Castle several hours away. There, they handed Andre over to Lieutenant-Colonel John Jameson, commanding Sheldon's dragoon regiment. Jameson, glancing over the papers, unsuspectingly agreed at Andre's request, to send him on to Arnold at West Point. But Major Benjamin Tallmadge, the head of Washington's spy ring, suspecting something wrong, ordered Andre brought back.

Arnold, preparing to have breakfast with General Washington, learned about Andre's arrest the next morning. Kissing Peggy, who fainted on the floor, Arnold galloped downstairs, saddled a horse, and fled to the Hudson River, where he boarded the *HMS Vulture*. The news of Benedict's Arnold's betrayal soon went public. The American officers, while despising Arnold's treason, felt much sympathy for the unfortunate Andre. Washington wrote to Clinton, assuring that he would release his favorite aide if Clinton handed Arnold over to him. Clinton refused.

Andre then went before a military tribunal. Despite the evident sympathy for Andre among Washington's high command, General Clinton refused to deliver up Arnold, sealing Andre's fate. At noon on October 2, 1780, American soldiers escorted Major Andre to the gallows at Tappan, New York. He had requested to be shot honorably, as a soldier, but Washington refused. He would be hanged as a spy. Wearing his regimental uniform and boots, he calmly tied the handkerchief over his own eyes and arranged the noose around his neck just moments before his death. Finally, he spoke: "I pray you to bear me witness that I meet my fate like a brave man." He was thirty years old. Many of the officers present had tears in their eyes. After Andre's death, the soldiers found a religious poem that he had written hidden in his pocket.

John Paulding, David Williams, and Isaac Van Wart, three Westchester patriots who had captured Andre received two hundred dollars in annual pensions, impressive farms in New York State, and a medal known as the Fidelity Medallion. Despite their fame during their lifetimes, many still felt much sympathy for Andre's fate, believing that the three men had simply stopped him to search him for valuables. Everyone but Andre, in fact, seemed to profit from the whole affair. The British rewarded Benedict Arnold with a brigadier general's commission and an annual income of several hundred

Monument to Major Andre

pounds. In the aftermath of Andre's death, Benedict Arnold escaped to the *HMS Vulture* on the Hudson River and went over to the British side. For the remainder of the war, he led 1,600 Loyalist troops into Virginia to raid the countryside. He died an old, penniless man, unloved as much as Andre had been admired and pitied.

On October 18, 1780, the Continental Congress issued its last decree: a Proclamation for a Day of Public Prayer recognizing the hand of Providence in discovering Benedict Arnold's treason. The three patriots had demonstrated alertness by uncovering Benedict Arnold's plot to hand over West Point to the British and thus averted disaster for the Patriot cause.

Bring me my American uniform, he ordered; and when they put it into his hands, he said: *I wish I had never changed it for another.*

Let me die in this old uniform in which I fought my battles. May God forgive me for ever having put on another.

—*Benedict Arnold,* dying words

Questions

1. Why did Benedict Arnold decide to betray his country? How much money was he to receive in exchange for his betrayal?
2. How did Arnold act treacherously? What was his plan?
3. How were his plans thwarted?
4. How did the three Patriots demonstrate alertness?
5. How did Major Benjamin Tallmadge practice alertness?
6. What was Major Andre's part in the scheme?
7. Was Arnold respected by the British for his treachery?
8. Where did Andre hide the papers?
9. How was God's Hand of Providence shown in discovering Arnold's treason?

Loyalty

DEFINITION

Committed to the welfare of those I serve, even to the detriment of my own comfort

MEMORY VERSE

Greater love hath no man thanthis, that a man lay down his life for his friends.

John 15:13

Swamp Fox

Col. Francis Marion

Snow's Island, South Carolina
Autumn, 1780

Two unkempt American scouts out on patrol picked him up as he pushed through the dense green canebrake and boggy ground near the Pee Dee River. Suddenly, they had slipped out of the undergrowth, one on each side of him, startling the young British officer with their silent, deer-like footsteps. As winter birds racketed overhead on their flight south, he spoke up, informing them that he was on his way to meet with Colonel Francis Marion, leader of the patriot guerrillas in South

General Marion invites the British officer to dinner

Carolina, to discuss a prisoner exchange. Instantly, they slipped a blindfold over his eyes and knotted it, shutting out the world in blackness. Stumbling as he tried to follow them, the young British officer realized that no other man in Cornwallis' army had seen the Americans' secret camp.

As Marion's scouts pushed deeper into the Pee Dee swamp, the young British officer could not understand what made these men live out here for months at a time. He wondered if they were taking him to their leader. But the blindfold and their silence did not allow for much talking. The scouts poled their boat under giant bald cypress trees until they came to a long, low ridge about five miles long and two miles wide. They had reached Snow's Island. Here, the partisans stockpiled weapons, ammunition, and what provisions they could scavenge or hunt. Trees stood knee-deep in swamp water that bred clouds of mosquitoes. A lake to the west protected the camp. The officer had heard that Marion's men kept British prisoners somewhere on the island.

Abruptly, the blindfold was removed and the British officer saw a small fire burning under a canopy of huge old trees. Groups of ragged men stood around. He wondered which one of the men was Colonel Francis Marion, famed leader of a band of American partisan fighters. Then he saw a short, lean man clad in stained deerskin clothes dismounting with difficulty from horseback. A manservant helped lift the man from his horse. As he started towards the British officer, the Redcoat could see that he limped heavily, his ankle twisted from a badly-healed break a year before. Close-up, Colonel Francis Marion's jutting chin and dark featured face showed the effects of a rough frontier life and constant danger.

After greeting each other, Francis Marion and the British officer drew aside to discuss the exchange of British prisoners on the island, while dinner cooked.

Serving under Captain William Moultrie in a brutal war against the Cherokee in 1757, Francis Marion, a South Carolina plantation owner, had learned the value of ambush and concealment. He understood how to use the lay of the land to attack without warning, unlike British soldiers who floundered through the swamps at the mercy of every Native American arrow or gun.

Marion's independent unit, consisting of twenty to thirty men, became known for their swift hit-and-run tactics when the focus of the Revolutionary War shifted from the northern to the southern colonies. On the morning of August 2, 1780, they ambushed a British camp at Nelson's Ferry on the upper Santee River, freeing one hundred fifty American prisoners. Marion lost only one man who was killed and another wounded. As 10,000 British soldiers under General Charles Cornwallis occupied Savannah, much of the Georgia colony and then marched on Charleston, Marion's guerillas struck again. They struck when least suspected, hitting British supply lines and harrying lonely outposts near the Great and Little Pee Dee Rivers. Increasingly alarmed at these phantom attacks, Cornwallis sent the Tory militia after the patriots. But the Loyalists failed to catch Marion. Throughout the fall of 1780, his victories piled up. Flitting among the swamps like a wily ghost, Marion defeated the British at Blue Savannah, Black Mingo Creek, and Tearcoat Swamp. When Major Patrick

Colonel Banastre Tarleton

Ferguson's troops suffered a devastating defeat at King's Mountain in mid-October, Cornwallis decided that Marion had to be stopped.

British Lieutenant Colonel Banastre Tarleton, known for his policy of "No Quarter," took up the chase. Pouncing upon Marion's camp at Ox Swamp, Tarleton thought that he had successfully flushed his quarry. As Tarleton's cavalry gave chase, they expected to quickly snare the guerrillas. But Marion and his men somehow kept so far ahead of the British troopers that they never even caught a glimpse of their horse's tails. For seven hours and across twenty-six rugged miles, Tarleton pursued the partisan leader. Finally, after struggling futilely through heavy swamplands, the British colonel gave up.

"As for this … old fox," Tarleton snapped, "the Devil himself could not catch him." With these words, Francis Marion rode into history as the "Swamp Fox."

As Marion and the British officer finished discussing the prisoner exchange, the smell of cooking filled the air. Turning to the young officer, Marion asked him to stay and have dinner with them. Surprised at the invitation, the officer agreed and sat down. Soon Oscar, Marion's black manservant, called out that dinner was ready. He dug into the hot ashes and dished up the meal. Provisions sometimes included hominy, cornmeal, molasses, fish, wild hogs when they could catch them, and the tough, stringy beef cattle that roamed the swamp. Marion's men served the British officer first. One of them dipped up a mug of swamp water. Another man handed him a bark plate. It held several small roasted sweet potatoes. Astonished, the British officer looked into the pinched faces of the men around the fire.

General Francis Marion

"But surely," the officer objected, "this cannot be your ordinary fare."

"Indeed, sir, it is," Marion spoke up, dryly, "and we are fortunate on this occasion, entertaining company, to have more than our usual allowance."

Intrigued, the officer asked what his men were paid.

Nothing, they replied.

Deeply puzzled, the officer wanted to know why men would live on a starvation diet in the middle of a swamp unless they were paid to do it. What were they fighting for?

Marion gave a simple reply: Freedom.

The young officer stared at them, holding the bark plate in his hands. Unpaid, living off root vegetables and swamp water, and covered with mosquito bites, this motley militia of white settlers, slaves, and teenage boys expressed incredible loyalty to the cause of independence.

Even when supplies dwindled, Marion refused to let his men loot or plunder the region and issued orders to that effect. Men who took "Provisions or forage from any person or plantations without a written authority from me … will be Deemed plunderers & Suffer Accordingly and part[ie]s will be sent to destroy all such plunderers wherever they may be found."

If they had to requisition stock or horses, Marion's men always gave the owners a receipt which was faithfully paid to them when the war ended. Though caught up in a savage partisan war that frequently took its toll on the civilian population, including Marion's sixteen-year-old nephew, Gabriel, who was summarily executed by the British, Marion refused to take revenge. Without ever losing control of his irregular but well-disciplined force, he conducted operations strictly by the rules of warfare and courtesy.

When he heard this, the war ended for the British officer. After seeing these men face to face, he knew that he could never view them the same way again. Finishing his meal, the officer made his way back to Charleston, swearing never to fight against such devoted patriots. Francis Marion and his men demonstrated loyalty to their country by refusing to stop fighting for freedom even in the face of hardship and overwhelming odds.

It was by the power of love and not of terror that he managed his men. They loved him for himself, his rare command of temper, affectionate manner, calm superiority, confidence and his courage for the fight for the freedom of their country.

— *William Gilmore Simms,*

author, *Marion, The Life of Francis Marion*

Questions

1. Why was the British officer looking for Francis Marion?
2. Why did the men blindfold him?
3. Why did Francis Marion limp?
4. What was Marion's battle strategy? How many men did he command?
5. How many prisoners were freed at Nelson's Ferry?
6. For what was Tarlteton known?
7. How did Marion become known as the "Swamp Fox"?
8. How did Marion extend hospitality to the British officer?
9. What did they serve for dinner? What did they use for a plate?
10. How much were Marion's men paid?
11. For what reason did they tell the officer they fought?
12. Did Marion allow his men to loot and plunder?
13. How did being among such loyal Patriots affect the British officer?
14. How did Marion and his men exemplify loyalty?
15. How can you endeavor to show loyalty to your family? church? your country?

Boldness

DEFINITION

Facing confrontation with the assurance
that God will bless the outcome
if I'm standing firm for truth

MEMORY VERSE

And now, Lord, behold their threatenings:
and grant unto thy servants, that with all
boldness they may speak thy word …

Acts 4:29

Overmountain Men

Col. John Sevier

Blue Ridge Mountains, North Carolina
September 25–October 7, 1780

Note: "Overmountain Men" refers to the fact that their settlements were west of or "over" the Appalachians.

The message came over the mountains. Samuel Phillips, captured by British forces, staggered into his community in East Tennessee carrying a letter. The trees did not quiver across the Blue Ridge, but British Major Patrick Ferguson's voice carried clearly, menacingly. "If you do not lay down your arms, he warned, I will march over the mountains and 'lay waste the country with fire and sword.' " But no one spoke to the men from over the mountain like that. Their anger flared immediately. Not content with the fall of Charleston, South Carolina, or a string of British victories across the south, Lord Cornwallis intended to subdue the tough mountain patriots as well, and crush all patriot activities in the mountains. Already, Major Ferguson's detachment had hacked apart a small force under Charles McDowell, several days' march away.

Major Patrick Ferguson

Isaac Shelby, Samuel Phillips' cousin, galloped forty miles to Watauga to see thirty-five-year-old John "Nolichucky Jack" Sevier, frontiersman, colonel of the

Washington County Militia and future first governor of Tennessee. While women hastily packed food and clothing for the march, Sevier raised a militia to confront Ferguson. The Overmountain Men* grabbed muskets and lead balls as the Reverend Samuel Doak bellowed a fire and brimstone sermon against the British. Colonel Sevier borrowed funds for the expedition, even putting his own property on the line as collateral. On September 25th, Sevier, his two sons and three hundred neighbors gathered at Sycamore Shoals, a stony stretch of river rapids bordered by cane thickets. They set out from their farms across the mountains, fording the North Toe River and splitting up their troops when they reached Gillespie Gap on the eastern Blue Ridge.

Other militia forces linked up with them on the way. Sevier and his men moved down to North Cove to meet up with the ragtag remnants of McDowell's army. Quarrels broke out on the way between the various militia colonels as to which man should lead the combined militias. After sending a message off to General Horatio Gates' headquarters, Sevier and his fellow colonels elected William Campbell as nominal leader and agreed to lead as a council.

As the patriot forces, now swelled to a thousand, filed through Yellow Gap and wound their way up a rutted trail past the North Toe River, two militia deserters informed Ferguson that the Overmountain Men were on the move. After hesitating for three days, Ferguson finally decided to retreat. He ran for the safety of Cornwallis' army, camped at Charlotte, North Carolina. On the way, he stopped at Broad River to circulate yet another aggressive public letter, demanding that the local Loyalist militia join him rather than be humiliated by a "set of mongrels."

Colonel John Sevier

By early October, the Overmountain Men were hard on Ferguson's heels. Afraid that he had kicked a rattlesnake's nest with his threatening messages, Ferguson sent a letter to Cornwallis, begging for reinforcements. During the chase, the patriots managed to keep just one step behind. On October 4, they reached the ashes of Ferguson's camp at Gilbert Town. That same day, thirty Georgia mountain men, spoiling for a fight, joined them. Near the North and South Carolina border, another three or four hundred patriots fell into line with Sevier's men.

October 6 dawned. Locals whispered to Sevier that Ferguson had gone to the east, dashing towards Lord Cornwallis and Charlotte. The Overmountain Men set off in hot pursuit. If Ferguson reached the safety of Cornwallis' flank, they knew that they would either have to give up the chase or tangle with a much larger and better-equipped army. Meanwhile, patriot spies sent word that Ferguson had set up camp on top of King's Mountain, fifty miles from Charlotte. With him were 1,500 Loyalists. The Overmountain Men now numbered 1,400. Instead of quick-marching for the border, Ferguson decided to stop and rest for the night. It would prove a fatal mistake. While he scribbled yet another letter to Cornwallis, asking for more troops, the patriots kept marching through the night.

With Ferguson so close to the border, the Overmountain Men had to move fast. Mounting nine hundred men on horseback, they rode off towards King's Mountain. Slopping through the chilly October night and pouring rain, they waded through Broad River, just fifteen miles from the mountain, as the sun rose. King's Mountain rose from the earth like a monstrous human foot, sixty feet in the air, the heel jutted up, ending in a narrow instep and a giant round toe. The Loyalists, camped on the ridge west of King's Pinnacle, the highest point on the mountain, had not left yet. The patriots huddled at the bottom for a few moments, staring up at the rocky, forested mound. Having marched for thirteen days straight, they were half-starved, wet, and dirty.

While the Redcoats had the advantage of the higher ground, the lay of the land lent an element of surprise, as the Americans could scramble up the rocky gorges, unseen by the Redcoats above.

Together, the Overmountain Men formed a U-shaped line around the mountain. John Sevier and William Campbell led two groups to attack the thickly wooded "heel," while Winston and McDowell hit the south slope. Campbell yelled to his men to fight with all their might. At three p.m., both opened fire at once. John Crockett, father of Davy Crockett, helped lead the charge. Spreading out in parties of one or two hundred men, the patriots attacked the steep face. As gunshots echoed off the mountain, Captain Abraham DePeyster spun around to stare at Ferguson. "These things are ominous," he exclaimed. "These are the yelling boys!"

Ferguson was the only British officer in the entire militia, which included a handful of New York Loyalists dressed in bright red coats. Only eleven hundred men remained in camp at this moment. Trapped on top of the mountain and surrounded on all sides, Ferguson had not dug in or constructed any fortifications. Below them, eight parties under their colonels struck the main Loyalist body at the ball of the heel. On the south flank, Sevier's patriots tried to break the Loyalist line and failed.

The gathering of the Overmountain Men at Sycamore Shoals

Ferguson put himself at the head of a bayonet charge against Sevier, causing Sevier's troops, who had no bayonets, to tumble downhill in alarm. Stopping at the base of the mountain, their sharpshooters turned and fired upward. Ferguson led another charge, then another, in an endless cycle. The Overmountain Men lunged uphill as the Tories formed ranks and galloped down, herding the Americans before them. Then the patriots regrouped and scrambled uphill again. Colonel James Williams went down, fatally shot. Campbell was wounded. In the confusion, the Loyalists found it difficult to pin down their target as the patriots fought like Indians, darting among the trees and thickets for cover. In addition, the downward angle of the hill made the Loyalists shoot high over the patriots' heads.

An hour passed. The Loyalists had lost hundreds of militiamen, while the Overmountain Men had suffered fewer than thirty casualties. Ferguson galloped back and forth across the crest, blowing his silver whistle to give the signal to attack. But just then Sevier and his colonels made a flanking movement, sliding behind the Loyalist army, and struck Ferguson in the rear. Pushed back to their camp on the toe of the mountain, the Loyalists began dropping like flies. White surrender flags popped up everywhere. Ferguson rode along, chopping with his sword at any little white flags he saw go up. But he must have known that the end was near. Still, he shouted: "Hurrah, brave boys, the day is ours!" Only a few officers responded and with him tried to hack out of the Americans' ring. At that moment, a patriot volley erupted from the woods and Ferguson pitched out of the saddle with seven bullet wounds in his body.

Then everyone rushed to surrender. Captain DePeyster sent a man out with a white flag of truce, begging for quarter. But the Overmountain Men remembered how British Colonel Banastre Tarleton massacred so many of Abraham Buford's men at the Battle of Waxhaw after they had surrendered. Now, some chose not to take prisoners alive, while others did not realize in the chaos that the Loyalists had already surrendered. They knocked back DePeyster's white flag, yelling: "Give 'em Tarleton's Quarter!" and "Give them Buford's play!"

The American fire continued for the next few minutes. Just then, Colonel Sevier and the other officers ran forward and ordered the Overmountain Men to cease fire. Only seven hundred Loyalists were left. The battle had lasted sixty-five minutes. The Loyalists had lost two hundred forty-four killed, one hundred sixty-three wounded and six hundred sixty-eight taken prisoner. The Overmountain Men, on the other hand, had suffered only twenty-nine killed and fifty-eight wounded in over an hour's fighting. Sevier's brother Robert, however, lay on the ground, mortally wounded. The patriots hastily buried their dead in shallow graves. With the threat of Cornwallis' army looming over them, they had to leave the wounded men alone on top of King's Mountain.

In the battle's aftermath, judgment competed with mercy. A drumhead court tried and hanged nine Loyalists for treason against the colonies, desertion from patriot militias, and for inciting the Cherokee Indians. Over the next few days, all but one hundred thirty Loyalists escaped into the woods as the militia marched single-file through deeply wooded areas.

The victory at King's Mountain had broken the backbone of the Loyalists in the Carolina backcountry. They would never be a military force again. The brief, sharp victory at King's Mountain turned the tide of the war in the South. The Loyalists had possessed both superior forces and the advantage of the high ground. Yet John Sevier and his Overmountain Men defeated them in a little over an hour. Lord Cornwallis, scrapping his plans for an invasion of North Carolina, retreated from Charlotte across the South Carolina border. He would not attempt to break into North Carolina again until the following year. The boldness that John Sevier and the Overmountain Men demonstrated at King's Mountain gave a tremendous boost of morale to the patriot cause, changing the tide from defeat to victory.

Questions

1. Tell some instances in which the Overmountain Men demonstrated boldness.
2. How did the boldness shown by John Sevier and his men aid the American cause?
3. What decision did Major Ferguson make that benefited the American cause?
4. What distresses did the Overmountain Men experience in order to boldly advance to King's Mountain?
5. The Redcoats had the advantage of being on higher ground. What advantages did the Overmountain Men have?
6. How many casualties did the Redcoats have? What about Sevier's men?
7. Did Sevier choose to show revenge to Ferguson's men?
8. What were the results of the victory at King's Mountain concerning the freedom of North Carolina?
9. What situation do you now face that would encourage others if you faced it by demonstrating boldness?

Selected Bibliography

Adams, John, and L. H. Butterfield. *Diary and Autobiography of John Adams, Vol. II.* Cambridge: Harvard University Press, 1962.

Aldridge, Alfred O. *Benjamin Franklin and Nature's God.* Durham, NC: Duke University Press, 1967.

Allison, Robert. *The Boston Massacre.* Beverly, MA: Applewood Books, 2006.

Amler, Jane Frances. *Haym Solomon: Patriot Banker of the American Revolution.* Powerkids Press, 2004.

Ammon, Richard. *Valley Forge.* Holiday House, 2006.

Anderson, Fred. *Crucible of War: The Seven Years' War and the Fate of Empire in British North America: 1754-1766.* New York: Alfred A. Knopf, 2000.

Archer, Richard. *As if an Enemy's Country: the British Occupation of Boston and the Origins of Revolution.* Oxford, New York: Oxford University Press, 2010.

Barton, Charles D. *The Bulletproof George Washington.* Wallbuilders Press, 1990.

Barton, David. *The Jefferson Lies.* Thomas Nelson, 2012 (This is an excellent book and we highly recommend it. It is thoroughly documented and also dispels other myths about Jefferson so prevalently believed today.)

Beliles, Mark A. and Stephen K. McDowell. *America's Providential History.* Charlottesville, VA: Providence Foundation, 1989.

Bessette, Joseph M. and John J. Pitney, Jr. *American Government and Politics: Deliberation, Democracy and Citizenship.* Boston: Wadsworth Cengage Learning, 2011.

Billias, George Athan. *General John Glover and his Marblehead Mariners.* New York: Holt, Rinehart & Winston, 1960.

Bobrick, Benson. *Angel in the Whirlwind: The Triumph of the American Revolution.* New York: Simon & Schuster, 2011.

Bodie, Idella. *The Man Who Loved the Flag.* Heroes and Heroines of the American Revolution, 2008.

Bowdoin, James, Samuel Adams, et al. *A Short Narrative of the Horrid Massacre.* London: W. Bingley, 1770.

Bowen, Catherine Drinker. *Miracle at Philadelphia: The Story of the Constitutional Convention: May to September 1787.* New York: Book-of-the-Month Club, Inc., 1986.

Boyd, Julian P. and Gerard W. Gawalt. *The Declaration of Independence: The Evolution of the Text.* University Press of New England, 1999.

Brady, Patricia. *Martha Washington: An American Life.* New York: Viking Press, 2005.

Brandt, Clare. *The Man in the Mirror: A Life of Benedict Arnold.* New York: Random House, 1994.

Brookhiser, Richard. *James Madison*. Basic Books, 2011.

Brooks, Victor. *The Boston Campaign*. Conshohocken, PA: Combined Publishing, 1999.

Buchanan, John. *The Road to Valley Forge: How Washington Built the Army that Won the Revolution*. Wiley: 2004.

Burnett, Edward Cody. *The Continental Congress*. New York: Norton, 1941.

Burnham, Norman Hammond. *The Battle of Groton Heights: A Story of the Storming of Fort Griswold and the Burning of New London, on the Sixth of September, 1781*. Kessinger Publishing, 2006.

Carbone, Gerald M. *Nathanael Greene: A Biography of the American Revolution*. New York: Palgrave Macmillan, 2010.

Carstens, Kenneth C. and Nancy Son Carstens, eds. *The Life of George Rogers Clark, 1752-1818: Triumphs and Tragedies*. Westport, CT: Praeger, 2004.

Cheney, Lynne. *When Washington Crossed the Delaware: A Wintertime Story for Young Patriots*. New York: Simon & Schuster, 2012.

Chernow, Ron. *Washington: A Life*. New York: Penguin Press, 2010.

Clary, David A. *George Washington's First War: His Early Military Adventures*. New York: Simon & Schuster, 2011.

Coffin, Charles L. *The Boys of '76*. Weiner Media, 2009.

Collier, Christopher. *Decision in Philadelphia: The Constitutional Convention of 1787.* New York: Ballantine Books, 2007.

Collins, Kathleen. *Marquis de Lafayette: French Hero of the American Revolution.* Rosen Central, 2004.

Connecticut Society of the Sons of the American Revolution. *King George's Head.* Sons of the American Revolution, Winter, 1998.

Cooley, Timothy Mather. *Sketches of the Life and Character of the Reverend Samuel Haynes, A.M., for Many Years Pastor of a Church in Rutland, Vermont, and Late in Granville, New York.* New York: Negro Universities Press, 1969.

Copp, John J. *The Battle of Groton Heights: The Massacre of Fort Griswold; and the Burning of New London.* Groton Heights Centennial Committee, 1879.

Crocker, Thomas E. *Braddock's March: How the Man Sent to Seize a Continent Changed American History.* Westholme Publishing, 2011.

Crofut, W. A. and John M. Morris. *The Military and Civil History of Connecticut during the War of 1861-65.* Ledyard Bill, 1868.

Dameron, J. David. *Kings Mountain: The Defeat of the Loyalists, October 7, 1780.* Cambridge, MA: DaCapo Press, 2003.

Davis, Burke. *Black Heroes of the American Revolution.* Sandpiper, 1992.

Dawson, Thomas Fulton. *Life and Character of Edward Oliver Wolcott, Late a Senator of the United States From the State of Colorado.* Forgotten Books, 2012.

Derleth, August. *Vincennes: Portal to the West.* Englewood Cliffs, New Jersey: Prentice-Hall, 1968.

Dorson, Richard M., *Patriots of the American Revolution: True Accounts by Great Americans from Ethan Allen to George Rogers Clark.* New York: Gramercy Books, 1953.

Driver, Carl S. *John Sevier: Pioneer of the Old Southwest.* Chapel Hill: University of North Carolina Press, 1932.

Dunkerly, Robert M. *The Battle of King's Mountain: Eyewitness Accounts.* The History Press, 2007.

Field, Joseph E. *"Worthy Partner": The Papers of Martha Washington.* Praeger Press, 1994.

Finger, John R. *Tennessee Frontiers: Three Regions in Transition.* Indiana University Press, 2001.

Fischer, David Hackett. *Paul Revere's Ride.* New York: Oxford University Press, 1994.

—. *Washington's Crossing.* Oxford University Press, 2006.

Fleming, Thomas. *Washington's Secret War: The Hidden History of Valley Forge.* Harper Perennial, 2006.

Flexner, James Thomas. *The Traitor and the Spy: Benedict Arnold and John Andre.* New York: Little, Brown & Company, 1975.

Foreman, Samuel A. *Dr. Joseph Warren: The Boston Tea Party, Bunker Hill, and the Birth of American Liberty.* New York: Pelican Publishing, 2011.

Freedman, Russell. *Washington at Valley Forge.* Holiday House: 2008.

Frothingham, Richard. *The Life and Times of Joseph Warren.* Applewood Books, 2009.

Fritz, Jean. *Why Not Lafayette?* New York: Puffin, 2001.

Garrison, Webb. *White House Ladies: Fascinating Tales and Colorful Curiosities.* Tennessee: Thomas Nelson Press, 1996.

Gingrich, Newt. *Valley Forge.* St. Martin's Griffin, 2011.

Golway, Terry. *Washington's General: Nathanael Greene and the Triumph of the American Revolution.* New York: Holt, 2005.

Goodrich, Charles A. *Lives of the Signers to the Declaration of Independence.* New York: Thomas Mather, 1832.

Gordon, William. *The History of the Rise, Progress, and Establishment, of the Independence of the United States of America.* Berkeley: University of California Collection, 1788.

Greene, George W. *The Life of Nathanael Greene, Major-General in the Army of the Revolution.* 3 vols. Freeport, NY: Books for Libraries Press, 1972.

Hall, Verna M. *The Christian History of the Constitution of the United States of America.* San Francisco: Foundation for American Christian Education, 1983.

Hanna, Willard A. *The Berkshire–Litchfield Legacy.* C. E. Tuttle and Company, 1984.

Harrison, Lowell H. *George Rogers Clark and the War in the West.* Lexington, KY: University of Kentucky Press, 2001.

Hatch, Robert McConnell. *Major John Andre: A Gallant in Spy's Clothing.* New York: Houghton Mifflin, 1986.

Haugen, Brenda. *Martha Washington: First Lady of the United States.* Compass Point Books, 2005.

Haw, James. " 'Every Thing Here Depends upon Opinion': Nathanael Greene and Public Support in the Southern Campaigns of the American Revolution." *South Carolina Historical Magazine,* 109 (July 2008): 212-31.

Heinemann, Ronald L., John G. Kolp, Anthony S. Parent, Jr., and William G. Shade. *Old Dominion, New Commonwealth: A History of Virginia, 1607-2007.* University of Virginia Press, 2007.

Hibbert, Christopher. *Redcoats and Rebels: The War for America 1770-1781.* Grafton Books, 1990

Hobson, Charles F. and Robert A. Rutlands, eds. *The Papers of James Madison: Volume 12, 2 March 1789-20 January 1790.* Charlottesville: University Press of Virginia, 1979.

Hogeland, William. *Declaration: The Nine Tumultuous Weeks When America Became Independent, May 1–July 4, 1776.* New York: Simon & Schuster, 2010.

Hutchinson, Francis. *A Fair Account of the Late Unhappy Disturbance at Boston.* London: B. White, 1770.

Isaacson, Walter. *Benjamin Franklin: An American Life.* New York: Simon & Schuster, 2004.

Jefferson, Thomas. *Jefferson's "Bible"; The Life and Morals of Jesus of Nazareth XV-XVI.* ed. Judd Patton (Grove City): American Book Distributors, 1996.

Jefferson, Thomas. *The Writings of Thomas Jefferson, Vol. 9.* ed. Paul Leicester Ford. New York: G.P. Putnam's Sons, 1899.

Johnson, Clifton (1915). *The Picturesque Hudson.* MacMillan. Retrieved 2009-07-08.

Jones, Charles Colcock. *Sergeant William Jasper.* Kessinger Publishing, 2010

Kaplan, Sidney, and Emma Nogrady Kaplan. *The Black Presence in the Era of the American Revolution.* Amherst, MA: The University of Massachusetts Press, 1989.

Ketcham, Ralph Louis. *James Madison: A Biography.* Charlottesville, VA: University of Virginia Press, 1971.

Ketchum, Richard M. *Saratoga: Turning Point of America's Revolutionary War.* New York: Henry Holt, 1997.

Kopperman, Paul. *Braddock at the Monongahela.* Pittsburgh, PA: University of Pittsburgh Press, 1977.

Krensky, Stephen. *DK Biography: Benjamin Franklin.* DK Children: 2007.

Labunski, Richard. *James Madison and the Struggle for the Bill of Rights.* New York, NY: Oxford University Press, 2006.

Lane, Jason. *General and Madame de Lafayette: Partners in Liberty's Cause in the American and French Revolutions.* Taylor Trade Publishing, 2003.

Lindenmeyer, Otto. *Black & Brave: The Black Soldier in America.* New York, 1970.

Loane, Nancy K. *Following the Drum: Women at the Valley Forge Encampment.* Potomac Books, Inc., 2009.

Lockhart, Paul Douglas. *The Drillmaster of Valley Forge: the Baron de Von Steuben and the Making of the American Army.* New York: Harper Collins, 2008.

Lodge, Henry Cabot and Theodore Roosevelt. *Hero Tales from American History,* George Grant, ed. White Hall, WV: Tolle Lege Press, 2012.

Luzader, John F. *Saratoga: A Military History of the Decisive Campaign of the American Revolution.* New York: Savas Beatie, 2010.

Maier, Pauline. *American Scripture: Making the Declaration of Independence.* New York: Knopf, 1997.

Marshall, Peter and David Manuel. *The Light and the Glory.* Revell, 1977.

Martin, James Kirby. *Benedict Arnold, Revolutionary War Hero: An American Warrior Reconsidered.* New York: New York University Press, 1997.

Massachusetts Historical Society. *Henry Knox Diary, 20 November 1775 to 13 January 1776.*

Massey, Gregory D. *General Nathanael Greene and the American Revolution in the South.* University of South Carolina Press, 2012.

McClung, Robert. *Young George Washington and the French and Indian War, 1753-1758.* Linnet Books, 2002.

McCrady, Edward. *The History of South Carolina in the Revolution, 1775-1780.* New York: Macmillan, 1901.

McCullough, David. *1776.* New York: Simon & Schuster, 2005.

Messick, Hank. *King's Mountain: The Epic of the Blue Ridge "Mountain Men" in the American Revolution.* New York: Little & Brown, 1976.

Middlekauff, Robert. *The Glorious Cause: The American Revolution, 1763-1789.* New York and Oxford: Oxford University Press, 2007.

Milgrim, Shirley Gorson. *Haym Salomon: Liberty's Son.* The Jewish Publication Society, 1979.

Mintz, Max M. *The Generals of Saratoga: John Burgoyne and Horatio Gates.* New Haven, CT: Yale University Press, 1990.

Morrissey, Brendan. *Saratoga 1777: Turning Point of a Revolution.* Oxford: Osprey Publishing, 2000.

Morrill, Dan. *Southern Campaigns of the American Revolution.* Nautical & Aviation Publishing, 1993.

National Archives Education Staff. *The Constitution: Evolution of a Government.* Santa Barbara: ABC-CLIO, Inc., 2001.

Pancake, John. *This Destructive War.* University of Alabama Press, 1985.

Payan, Gregory. *Marquis de Lafayette: French Hero of the American Revolution.* The Rosen Publishing Group, 2002.

Peacock, Louise. *Crossing the Delaware: A History in Many Voices.* Aladdin, 2007.

Peters, Madison C. *Haym Salomon: The Financier of the Revolution.* University Press of the Pacific, 2005.

Puls, Mark. *Henry Knox: Visionary General of the American Revolution.* New York: Palgrave, 2010.

Randall, Henry Stephens. *The Life of Thomas Jefferson,* Vol. 3. New York: Derby & Jackson, 1858.

Randall, William Sterne. *Benedict Arnold: Patriot and Traitor.* Dorset Press, 2001.

Randall, Williard Sterne. *Ethan Allen: His Life and Times.* New York: W. W. Norton, 2011.

Reit, Seymour. *Guns for General Washington: A Story of the American Revolution.* Sandpiper, 2001.

Rosen, Gary. *American Compact: James Madison and the Problem of Founding.* Lawrence, KS: University Press of Kansas, 1999.

Russell, Charles Edward. *Haym Solomon and the Revolution.* Ayer Company Publishers, 1930.

Rutland, Robert Allen. *James Madison: The Founding Father.* Columbia, MO: University of Missouri Press, 1987.

Saillant, John. *Black Puritan, Black Republican: The Life and Thought of Lemuel Haynes, 1753-1833.* New York: Oxford University Press, 2003.

Savas, Theodore P., and Dameron, J. David. *A Guide to the Battles of the American Revolution.* Savas Beatie, 2005.

Scheer, George F. and Hugh F. Rankin, *Rebels and Redcoats.* New York: The World Publishing Company, 1957.

Schwartz, Laurens R. *Jews and the American Revolution: Haym Solomon and Others,* Jefferson, NC: McFarland & Co., 1987.

Scollay, Mercy to Elijah Dix. "I Wear a Face Foreign to the Feelings of My Heart" (Boston: April 26, 1776). *Mercy Scollay Papers, 1775-1824.* Cambridge, MA: Cambridge Historical Society.

Silverman, Jerry. *Of Thee I Sing.* Citadel Press, 2002.

Silvey, Anita. *Henry Knox: Bookseller, Soldier, Patriot.* Clarion Books, 2010.

Simpson, Andrew. "In St. Patrick's Shadow: The Peculiar Holiday of Evacuation Day," *The Bostonian Society News* (2004, Issue 1).

Steele, William O. *John Sevier: Pioneer Boy. The Childhood of Famous Americans Series.* Indianapolis: Bobbs-Merrill, 1953.

Stewart, David O. *The Summer of 1787: The Men Who Invented the Constitution.* New York: Simon & Schuster, 2008.

Sumner Letter, "Boston 1775," accessed on 02/08/2013.

Tonsetic, Robert. *1781: The Decisive Year of the Revolutionary War.* Casemate, 2011.

Uhlar, Janet. *Liberty's Martyr: The Story of Dr. Joseph Warren.* Dog Ear Publishing, 2009.

Unger, Harlow Giles. *Lafayette.* Hoboken, NJ: John Wiley & Sons, 2002.

Vile, John R. *The Constitutional Convention of 1787: A Comprehensive Encyclopedia of America's Founding.* 2 Vols. ABC-CLIO: 2005.

Walett, Francis. "James Bowdoin, Patriot Propagandist." *The New England Quarterly:* 23:3 (September 1950).

Ware, Susan. *Forgotten Heroes: Inspiring American Portraits from Our Leading Historians.* Portland, OR: Simon & Schuster, 2000.

Warren, Joseph. *The Suffolk Resolves,* September 9, 1774.

Washington, George to Martha Washington, "My Dearest Life and Love," June 24, 1776.

Washington, George to William Gordon. "8 July 1788." *Writings,* 27: 49-52.

Wheeler, Richard "Little Bear." *God's Mighty Hand: Providential Occurrences in World History,* Bulverde, TX: Mantle Ministries Press.

Wheeler, William Bruce, Susan Becker, and Lorri Glover. *Discovering the American Past: A Look at the Evidence: To 1877.* Belmont, CA: Cengage Learning, 2011.

White, Alain C. *The History of the Town of Litchfield, Connecticut, 1720-1920.* Litchfield, CT: Enquirer Print, 1920.

White, Richard. *Jordan Freeman Was My Friend.* Xlibris Corps, 2003 (Historical Fiction).

Wilson, Barry K. *Benedict Arnold: A Traitor in Our Midst.* McGill Queens Press, 2001.

York, Neil Longley. *The Boston Massacre: A History with Documents.* New York: Taylor & Francis, 2010.

Websites and Other Media

Brennan, Daniel. "Did James Madison suffer a nervous collapse due to the intensity of his studies?" Mudd Manuscript Library Blog, January 2008, Princeton University Archives and Public Policy Papers Collection, Princeton University.

Fowler, William M. "Glover, John." *American National Biography Online,* www.anb.org/ February 2000.

Garden, Alexander. *"Sergeant Jasper, 2nd Regiment." Anecdotes of the Revolutionary War in America. 1822.* http://books.google.com/books?id=WJ98ynQ-W-AC&pg=PA90

"Henry Knox and the 'Noble Train of Artillery' " on the *Fort Ticonderoga National Historic Landmark* http://www.fort-ticonderoga.org/history/bibliographies/henry_knox.htm

"Heralds of a Liberal Faith," Volumes I-IV. http://harvardsquarelibrary.org/Heralds/Jonathan-Mayhew.php

Sevier, William Jay, and Lance Sevier. "The Life of John Sevier Time Line, Including Family Origins & World Events, 1506 -1815." http://www.johnsevier.com/jstime.html

"Saratoga National Historical Park." National Park Service. http://www.nps.gov/sara/.

(Documentary DVD) *Von Steuben's Continentals: The First American Army* (Actor: John D. Pagano, Lionheart Filmworks, 2007).

Photo credits

Alertness

Benedict Arnold: Public Domain. http://ushistoryimages.com/benedict-arnold.shtm

Mrs. Benedict Arnold: Public Domain. http://www.archives.gov/research/military/american-revolution/pictures/index.html#ne

Smith's House: Public Domain. http://freepages.history.rootsweb.ancestry.com/~wcarr1/Lossing1/Chap30.html

Fidelity Medallion: Public Domain. http://en.wikipedia.org/wiki/File:FidelityMedallion.jpg

Location of Andre's capture: Public Domain. http://freepages.history.rootsweb.ancestry.com/~wcarr1/Lossing1/Chap32.html

Death of Major Andre: Public Domain. http://www.archives.gov/research/military/american-revolution/pictures/index.html#ne

Boldness

John Sevier: Public Domain. http://en.wikipedia.org/wiki/File:John_Sevier.jpg

Isaac Shelby: Public Domain. http://en.wikipedia.org/wiki/File:Isaac_shelby.jpg

Gathering of Overmountain Men: Public Domain.Gathering of the Mountain Men at Sycamore Shoals, painting by Lloyd Branson, http://en.wikipedia.org/wiki/File:Gathering-of-overmountain-men-branson-tn1.jpg

Major Patrick Ferguson: Public Domain. http://sphotos-a.xx.fbcdn.net/hphotos-ash3/c0.0.403.403/p403x403/556487_350945968326921_740831943_n.jpg

Bravery

Col. Moultrie: Public Domain. http://www.archives.gov/research/military/american-revolution/pictures/index.html#portrait

Attack on Ft. Sullivan (Ft. Moultrie): Public Domain. http://ushistoryimages.com/major-battles-during-revolutionary-war.shtm

Jasper raising flag: Public Domain. http://en.wikipedia.org/wiki/File:Battle_of_Sullivans_Island.jpg

Siege of Savannah, Georgia: Public Domain. http://ushistoryimages.com/major-battles-during-revolutionary-war.shtm

Commitment

Portrait of Lafayette: http://www.lafayette.edu/about/files/2010/08/Marquis_banner.jpg

Lafayette and Washington at Valley Forge: http://colonialwilliamsburgbound.blogspot.com/2011/02/le-marquis-de-lafayette-un-heros-de-la.html

Lafayette at Mount Vernon: Public Domain. http://en.wikipedia.org/wiki/File:Washington_and_Lafayette_at_Mount_Vernon,_1784_by_Rossiter_and_Mignot,_1859.jpg

Lafayette rallying troops at Brandywine: Public Domain. http://ushistoryimages.com/major-battles-during-revolutionary-war.shtm

Treaty of Paris: http://www.estudiesweekly.com/images/pubimages/485/2237/Treaty%20of%20Paris.jpg

Compassion

Martha Washington Portrait: Public Domain. http://upload.wikimedia.org/wikipedia/commons/a/af/Martha_Washington_at_National_Portrait_Gallery_IMG_4487.JPG

George and Martha at Valley Forge: Public Domain. http://americangallery.wordpress.com/2009/07/14/tompkins-harrison-matteson-1813-1884/

"Before the Dawn": Public Domain. http://americangallery.wordpress.com/category/ferris-jlg/

Creativity

James Caldwell: Public Domain. http://greensleeves.typepad.com/berkshires/knyphausens_raid_1780/

Battle of Springfield: Public Domain. http://upload.wikimedia.org/wikipedia/commons/4/45/Battle_of_Springfield_NJ_1780.jpg

Discretion

Whaleboat: Public Domain. http://commons.wikimedia.org/wiki File:Whaleboat_Beechley_point_1950_corp1144.jpg

Benjamin Tallmadge: Pictorial Field Book of the Revolution http://freepages.history.rootsweb.ancestry.com/~wcarr1/Lossing1/Chap55.html

Clothesline: MorgueFile -file5951280048114.jpg

Loyalty

Swamp Fox: U.S. Capitol, "The Swamp Fox," John Blake White, oil on canvas, 1810

Col. Banastre Tarleton: Public Domain. http://en.wikipedia.org/wiki/File:Banastre-Tarleton-by-Joshua-Reynolds.jpg

General Francis Marion: Public Domain. http://www.nndb.com/people/107/000095819/

Orderliness

Von Steuben portrait: Public Domain. http://commons.wikimedia.org/wiki/File:Baron_von_Steuben_by_Ralph_Earl.jpeg

Suffering troops: Public Domain. http://ushistoryimages.com/valley-forge.shtm

Von Steuben training troops: Public Domain. Painting by Edwin Austin Abbey (1852-1911) http://usarmy.vo.llnwd.net/e2/-images/2009/06/14/37868/

Grand Parade of trained troops: Public Domain. http://www.revolutionaryday.com/usroute202/valleyforge/default.htm

Blue Book: Public Domain. http://www.army.mil/article/29717/After_230_years__the___039_Blue_Book__039__still_guides_NCOs/

Persistence

Fort Massac: Public Domain. http://en.wikipedia.org/wiki/File:Fort_Massac_IL_2.JPG

Four paintings of GR Clark: Public Domain. National Archives: http://www.archives.gov/research/military/american-revolution/pictures/index.html#ne. Paintings by Ezra Winter.

George R. Clark Portrait: Public Domain. http://cincinnati.com/blogs/ourhistory/2012/07/04/revolutionary-war-was-fought-locally/

Endnotes

[1]David Barton, The Role of Pastors and Christians, quoting Reports of Committees of the House of Representatives made During the First Session of the Thirty-third Congress.

[2]George Washington, "Address of George Washington, President of the United States … Preparatory to His Declination" (Baltimore: George and Henry S. Keatinge, 1796), p. 22-23

About the Authors

Marilyn Boyer is the mother of fourteen children, all home schooled from kindergarten through high school. Her passion to train up her children in the character of Christ led her to create Character Concepts Curriculum, a character curriculum for kids of all ages to equip parents in raising children of integrity!

Her many character resources, as well as books on homeschooling and Christian parenting, are available online.

About the Authors

Grace Tumas Ehrman holds a degree in history from Liberty University. Her paper, "Warlords and Samurais: Japanese Interventionists in Siberia During the Russian Civil War, 1918-1922," won an award at the 2013 Phi Alpha Theta History Conference. She specializes in American and Russian history.